Modern crochet GARDEN

Stylish Flower & Succulent Patterns to Stitch in a Day

Amy Gaines

BETTER DAY BOOKS®

HAPPY · CREATIVE · CURATED

Modern Crochet Garden © 2023 by Amy Gaines and Better Day Books, Inc.

This book is a revised and expanded edition
of *Make a Crochet Garden* (2017) and
Quick Crochet with Flowers (2018), both published by
Leisure Arts, Inc., 104 Champs Blvd., STE 100, Maumelle, AR 72113-6738.

Leisure Arts has been inspiring the creative community since 1971 with
innovative craft products, books, and more! For more info, please visit
www.leisurearts.com.

Publisher: Peg Couch
Cover and Book Designer: Ashlee Wadeson
Production Designer: Lori Malkin Ehrlich
Senior Graphic Artist: Lora Puls
Graphic Artist (*Quick Crochet with Flowers*): Kellie McAnulty
Editor: Colleen Dorsey
Instructional/Technical Writer (*Make a Crochet Garden*): Lois J. Long
Instructional/Technical Writer (*Quick Crochet with Flowers*): Cathy Hardy
Photostylist: Lori Wenger
Photographer: Jason Masters

Library of Congress Control Number: 2022946123

ISBN: 978-0-7643-6134-0
Printed in China
First printing

Copublished by Better Day Books, Inc., and Schiffer Publishing, Ltd.

MIX
Paper | Supporting
responsible forestry
FSC® C104723

BETTER DAY BOOKS®

Better Day Books
P.O. Box 21462
York, PA 17402
Phone: 717-487-5523
Email: hello@betterdaybooks.com
www.betterdaybooks.com
@better_day_books

SCHIFFER
PUBLISHING

Schiffer Publishing
4880 Lower Valley Road
Atglen, PA 19310
Phone: 610-593-1777
Fax: 610-593-2002
Email: info@schifferbooks.com
www.schifferbooks.com

This title is available for promotional or commercial use, including special
editions. Contact info@schifferbooks.com for more information.

DEDICATION

For my father,
Danny Charles Bryant.
I miss you.

Contents

welcome

Whether you are a crochet enthusiast looking for fresh patterns, a crocheter looking for make-in-a-day projects, or a curious crafter looking to start a new hobby, you're going to love this book!

These 22 trendy flower, succulent, and cacti projects will inspire you to fill your home with soft, easy-to-care-for plants that will never die on you. You'll learn how to make a wide array of items, including wall décor, practical coasters, personal accessories, and more. Each project comes with detailed stitch instructions, a shopping list, the finished size, and the skill level. Also included are general crochet instructions, stitch diagrams, and yarn information. Best of all, each project is totally achievable in just a single day or afternoon.

The flower chapter starts with tutorials for making ten flowers and four leaves. After you have mastered these basic elements, you can move on to a variety of projects that are built using these elements. The succulent chapter provides a wide range of plant and cactus projects that are as sweet as they are soft.

Are you ready to green up your life? Let's get started!

Happy stitching,

Amy

Getting STARTED

Whether you're a crochet beginner or a seasoned veteran, take a few minutes to review the basic instructions on the following pages. We'll go over all the abbreviations, symbols, and terms that will be used throughout the book, which will allow you to demystify the instructions with ease and get crocheting. Also included are quick reference charts for hook sizes, yarn weights, and difficulty levels.

You'll be whipping up creative cacti and fantastic flowers in no time!

abbreviations

ch(s) = chain(s)
cm = centimeters
dc = double crochet(s)
hdc = half double crochet(s)
hdc2tog = half double crochet 2 together
hdc3tog = half double crochet 3 together
mm = millimeters
rnd(s) = round(s)
sc = single crochet(s)
sc2tog = single crochet 2 together
sc3tog = single crochet 3 together
slip st = slip stitch
sp(s) = space(s)
st(s) = stitch(es)
tr = treble crochet(s)
YO = yarn over

symbols & terms

★ — work instructions following ★ as many **more** times as indicated in addition to the first time.

( ) — work enclosed instructions **as many** times as specified by the number immediately following, **or** work all enclosed instructions in the stitch or space indicated, **or** contains explanatory remarks.

colon (:) — the number(s) given after a colon at the end of a row or round denote(s) the number of stitches or spaces you should have on that row or round.

Yarn Weight Names and Number	LACE 0	SUPER FINE 1	FINE 2	LIGHT 3	MEDIUM 4	BULKY 5	SUPER BULKY 6	JUMBO 7
Type of Yarns in Category	Fingering, size 10 crochet thread	Sock, Fingering, Baby	Sport, Baby	DK, Light Worsted	Worsted, Afghan, Aran	Chunky, Craft, Rug	Super Bulky, Roving	Jumbo, Roving
Crochet Gauge* Ranges in Single Crochet to 4" (10 cm)	32-42 sts**	21-32 sts	16-20 sts	12-17 sts	11-14 sts	8-11 sts	6-9 sts	5 sts and fewer
Advised Hook Size Range	Steel*** 6 to 8, regular hook B-1	B-1 to E-4	E-4 to 7	7 to I-9	I-9 to K-10½	K-10½ to M/N-13	M/N-13 to Q	Q and larger

*GUIDELINES ONLY: The chart above reflects the most commonly used gauges and hook sizes for specific yarn categories.

**Lace weight yarns are usually crocheted with larger hooks to create lacy openwork patterns. For this reason, a gauge range is difficult to determine. Always follow the gauge stated in your pattern.

***Steel crochet hooks are sized differently from regular hooks—the higher the number, the smaller the hook, which is the reverse of regular hook sizing.

gauge

Exact gauge is **essential** for proper size. Before beginning your project, make the sample swatch given in the individual instructions in the yarn and hook specified. After completing the swatch, measure it, counting your stitches and rows carefully.

If your swatch is larger or smaller than specified, **make another, changing hook size to get the correct gauge.** Keep trying until you find the size of hook that will give you the specified gauge.

CROCHET TERMINOLOGY

UNITED STATES		INTERNATIONAL
slip stitch (slip st)	=	single crochet (sc)
single crochet (sc)	=	double crochet (dc)
half double crochet (hdc)	=	half treble crochet (htr)
double crochet (dc)	=	treble crochet (tr)
treble crochet (tr)	=	double treble crochet (dtr)
double treble crochet (dtr)	=	triple treble crochet (ttr)
triple treble crochet (tr tr)	=	quadruple treble crochet (qtr)
skip	=	miss

CROCHET HOOKS

U.S.	B-1	C-2	D-3	E-4	F-5	G-6	7	H-8	I-9	J-10	K-10½	L-11	M/N-13	N/P-15	P/Q	Q	S
Metric – mm	2.25	2.75	3.25	3.5	3.75	4	4.5	5	5.5	6	6.5	8	9	10	15	16	19

●○○○ BEGINNER	Projects for first-time crocheters using basic stitches. Minimal shaping	
●●○○ EASY	Projects using yarn with basic stitches, repetitive stitch patterns, simple color changes, and simple shaping and finishing	
●●●○ INTERMEDIATE	Projects using a variety of techniques, such as basic lace patterns or color patterns, and midlevel shaping and finishing	
●●●● EXPERIENCED	Projects with intricate stitch patterns, techniques, and dimension, such as nonrepeating patterns, multicolor techniques, fine threads, small hooks, detailed shaping, and refined finishing	

markers

Markers are used to help distinguish the beginning of each round being worked. Place a 2" (5 cm) scrap piece of yarn before the first stitch of each round, moving the marker after each round is complete.

joining with sc

When instructed to join with sc, begin with a slip knot on hook. Insert hook in stitch or space indicated, YO and pull up a loop, YO and draw through both loops on hook.

adjustable loop

Wind yarn around two fingers to form a ring (*Fig. 1a*). Slide yarn off fingers and grasp the strands at the top of the ring (*Fig. 1b*). Insert hook from **front** to **back** into the ring, pull up a loop, YO and draw through loop on hook to lock ring (*Fig. 1c*) (st made does **not** count as part of beginning ch). Working around both strands, follow instructions to work sts in the ring, then pull yarn tail to close (*Fig. 1d*).

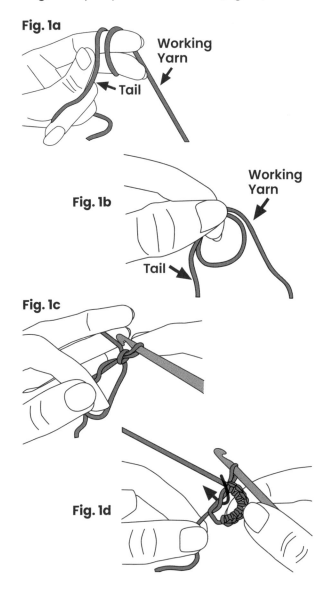

Fig. 1a

Working Yarn

Tail

Fig. 1b

Working Yarn

Tail

Fig. 1c

Fig. 1d

back or front loops only

Work only in loop(s) indicated by arrow (*Fig. 2*).

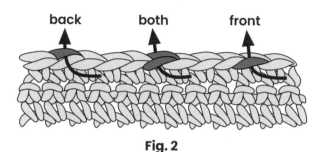

Fig. 2

free loops of a chain

When instructed to work in free loops of a chain, work in loop indicated by arrow (*Fig. 3*).

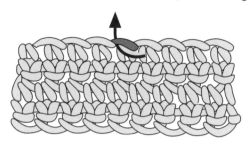

Fig. 3

straight stitch

Straight stitch is just what the name implies, a single, straight stitch. Come up at 1 and go down at 2 (*Fig. 4*).

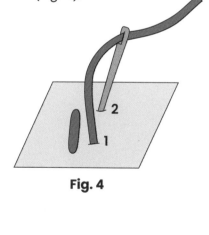

Fig. 4

whipstitch

With **wrong** side of piece together (or pieces if connecting two separate pieces), sew through both edges once to secure the beginning of the seam, leaving an ample yarn end to weave in later. Working through **both** loops of each stitch on **both** edges (*Fig. 5*), insert the needle from **front** to **back** and pull yarn through. ★ Bring the needle around and insert it from **front** to **back** through next stitch and pull yarn through; repeat from ★ across.

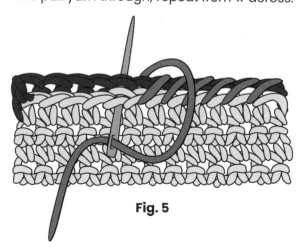

Fig. 5

fringe

Cut a piece of cardboard 5" (12.5 cm) wide and half as long as length of strands indicated in individual instructions. Wind the yarn loosely and evenly around the cardboard as many times as strands needed, then cut across one end.

Hold together as many strands as specified in individual instructions; fold in half.

With **wrong** side facing and using a crochet hook, draw the folded end up through a stitch or space and pull the loose ends through the folded end *(Fig. 6a)*; draw the knot up tightly *(Fig. 6b)*. Repeat, spacing as specified in individual instructions.

Lay piece on a hard surface and trim the ends.

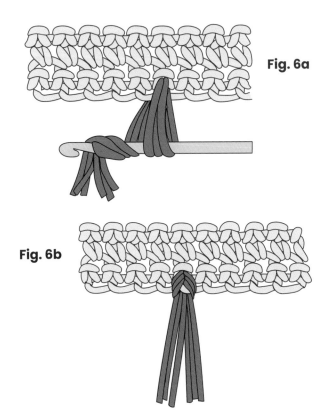

Fig. 6a

Fig. 6b

1

Splendid SUCCULENTS

There's no watering or upkeep needed with these wonderful home accents! You'll learn to make a miniature garden of lifelike, decorative cacti and succulents, from a prickly pear to a saguaro and more. Add the outdoors to any room!

You'll also learn to make useful cactus- and succulent-inspired home tools, such as a bowl for trinkets, a pencil cup holder, a potholder, and two different scrubbers.

Coaster
SET

This charming set of coasters—complete with its own pot to hold them in—will keep your drinks secure and your surfaces safe. Choose a yarn that makes sense for contact with wet or hot glasses and cups.

Yarn (Medium Weight)

(2.5 ounces, 120 yards [70.9 grams, 109 meters] per skein):

- Green: 1 skein
- Light Green: 1 skein
- Tan: 1 skein
- Peach: 5 yards (4.5 meters)
- Light Peach: 5 yards (4.5 meters)
- White: 5 yards (4.5 meters)

Crochet Hook

- Size G (4 mm)
  or size needed for gauge

Additional Supplies

- Yarn needle

Gauge Information

Each Coaster = 4" (10 cm) diameter

Make a gauge swatch that is 2" (5 cm) diameter. Work same as Coaster for 4 rnds: 24 sc.

 **EASY**

Approximate Finished Sizes:
Coaster: 4" (10 cm) diameter
Planter: 2" tall x 4¾" wide (5 cm x 12 cm)

coaster

(Make 3 **each** with Green and Light Green)

Rnd 1 (Right side)**:** With color indicated, make an adjustable loop to form a ring *(Figs. 1a-d, page 14)*, work 6 sc in ring; do **not** join, place marker to indicate beginning of rnd *(see Markers, page 14)*.

Note: Loop a short piece of yarn around any stitch to mark Rnd 1 as **right** side.

Rnd 2: 2 Sc in each sc around: 12 sc.

Rnd 3: (2 Sc in next sc, sc in next sc) around: 18 sc.

Rnd 4: (2 Sc in next sc, sc in next 2 sc) around: 24 sc.

Rnd 5: (2 Sc in next sc, sc in next 3 sc) around: 30 sc.

Rnd 6: (2 Sc in next sc, sc in next 4 sc) around: 36 sc.

Rnd 7: (2 Sc in next sc, sc in next 5 sc) around: 42 sc.

Rnd 8: (2 Sc in next sc, sc in next 6 sc) around; slip st in next sc, finish off.

flower

(Make 3 **each** with Peach and Light Peach)

With color indicated, ch 5.

Rnd 1 (Right side)**:** Slip st in fifth ch from hook, (ch 4, slip st in same ch as first slip st) 4 times; finish off leaving a long end for sewing.

Note: Mark Rnd 1 as **right** side.

planter

With Tan, ch 9.

Rnd 1 (Right side)**:** 2 Sc in second ch from hook, sc in next 6 chs, 4 sc in last ch; working in free loops of beginning ch *(Fig. 3, page 15)*, sc in next 6 chs, 2 sc in next ch; do **not** join, place marker to indicate beginning of rnd: 20 sc.

Note: Mark Rnd 1 as **right** side.

Rnd 2: 2 Sc in next sc, sc in next 8 sc, 2 sc in each of next 2 sc, sc in next 8 sc, 2 sc in next sc: 24 sc.

Rnd 3: Sc in back loop only of each sc around *(Fig. 2, page 15)*.

Rnd 4: Working in both loops, 2 sc in next sc, sc in next 10 sc, 2 sc in each of next 2 sc, sc in next 10 sc, 2 sc in next sc: 28 sc.

Rnd 5: 2 Sc in next sc, sc in next 12 sc, 2 sc in each of next 2 sc, sc in next 12 sc, 2 sc in next sc: 32 sc.

Rnd 6: 2 Sc in next sc, sc in next 14 sc, 2 sc in each of next 2 sc, sc in next 14 sc, 2 sc in next sc: 36 sc.

Rnd 7: 2 Sc in next sc, sc in next 16 sc, 2 sc in each of next 2 sc, sc in next 16 sc, 2 sc in next sc: 40 sc.

Rnd 8: Sc in each sc around; slip st in next sc, finish off.

BAND

With Tan, ch 43.

Row 1: Sc in second ch from hook and in each ch across: 42 sc.

Row 2 (Right side)**:** Ch 1, turn; sc in each sc across; finish off leaving a long end for sewing.

Note: Mark Row 2 as **right** side.

With **wrong** side together and long end, sew ends of Band together. Secure end; do **not** cut yarn.

With **wrong** side of Band and **right** side of Planter together, sew Band to Rnd 8 of Planter using same end; secure end.

Using photo as a guide for placement and using long ends, sew one Flower to each Coaster.

With White, add straight stitch *(Fig. 4, page 15)* "V" shapes to each Coaster as desired.

Dish SCRUBBER

This hardworking item will add a little fun to an otherwise tedious daily chore. The hanging loop makes it easy to hang it up to dry between uses.

Yarn (Medium Weight)

- Green: 40 yards (36.5 meters)
- Peach: small amount

Crochet Hook

- Size G (4 mm)

Additional Supplies

- Yarn needle

Gauge Information

Gauge is not of great importance; your Scrubber may be a little larger or smaller without changing the overall effect.

 **EASY**

Finished Size: Approximately 4" (10 cm) diameter, excluding hanger

scrubber

With Green and leaving a long end for sewing, ch 16.

Row 1 (Right side)**:** Sc in second ch from hook and in each ch across: 15 sc.

Note: Loop a short piece of yarn around any stitch to mark Row 1 as **right** side.

Rows 2–35: Ch 1, turn; sc in back loop only of each sc across *(Fig. 2, page 15)*.

Finish off leaving a long end for sewing.

Thread yarn needle with long end. With **wrong** side together and matching free loops of beginning ch *(Fig. 3, page 15)* to sts on Row 35, whipstitch piece together to form a tube *(Fig. 5, page 15)*.

Secure end, do **not** cut yarn. Weave needle through ends of rows, pull tightly to gather and secure end.

Thread yarn needle with beginning long end and weave needle through ends of rows; pull tightly to gather and secure end.

hanger

With Green, ch 12; finish off leaving a long end for sewing.

flower

With Peach, ch 6.

Rnd 1 (Right side)**:** Slip st in sixth ch from hook, (ch 5, slip st in same ch as first slip st) 4 times; finish off leaving a long end for sewing.

Note: Mark Rnd 1 as **right** side.

Using photo as a guide for placement and using long ends, sew Hanger and Flower to Scrubber.

Succulent GARDEN

This delicate and sweet hanging accessory will blend into and brighten any room of your home. Feel free to change up the colors of the hanger or bowl to coordinate with your décor.

Yarn (Medium Weight)

(3.5 ounces, 170 yards
[100 grams, 156 meters]
per skein):

- White: 1 skein
- Grey: 1 skein
- Fern: 1 skein
- Brown: 40 yards (36.5 meters)
- Sweet Pea: 20 yards
  (18.5 meters)
- Kelly Green: 15 yards
  (13.5 meters)
- Sage: 15 yards (13.5 meters)
- Yellow: small amount

Crochet Hook

- Size G (4 mm)
  or size needed for gauge

Additional Supplies

- Yarn needle
- Sewing needle and grey thread
- Polyester fiberfill
- Plastic poly pellets (optional)

Gauge Information

Make a gauge swatch that is 2¼" (5.75 cm) diameter. Work same as Planter for 4 rnds: 32 sc.

Stitch Guide

SINGLE CROCHET 2 TOGETHER *(abbreviated sc2tog)*
Pull up a loop in each of next 2 sc, YO and draw through all 3 loops on hook **(counts as one sc)**.

 **INTERMEDIATE**
Finished Size: 6" (15 cm) tall

planter

Rnd 1 (Right side)**:** With Grey, make an adjustable loop to form a ring *(Figs. 1a-d, page 14)*, work 8 sc in ring; do **not** join, place marker to indicate beginning of rnd *(see Markers, page 14)*.

Note: Loop a short piece of yarn around any stitch to mark Rnd 1 as **right** side.

Rnd 2: 2 Sc in each sc around: 16 sc.

Rnd 3: (2 Sc in next sc, sc in next sc) around: 24 sc.

Rnd 4: (2 Sc in next sc, sc in next 2 sc) around: 32 sc.

Rnd 5: (2 Sc in next sc, sc in next 3 sc) around: 40 sc.

Rnd 6: (2 Sc in next sc, sc in next 4 sc) around: 48 sc.

Rnd 7: (2 Sc in next sc, sc in next 5 sc) around: 56 sc.

Rnd 8: (2 Sc in next sc, sc in next 6 sc) around: 64 sc.

Rnd 9: (2 Sc in next sc, sc in next 7 sc) around: 72 sc.

Rnd 10: (2 Sc in next sc, sc in next 7 sc) around: 81 sc.

Rnds 11-18: Sc in each sc around.

Rnd 19: Sc in next sc, (sc2tog, sc in next 3 sc) around; slip st in next sc, finish off leaving a long end for sewing.

soil

Rnd 1 (Right side)**:** With Brown, make an adjustable loop to form a ring, work 6 sc in ring; do **not** join, place marker to indicate beginning of rnd.

Note: Mark Rnd 1 as **right** side.

Rnd 2: 2 Sc in each sc around: 12 sc.

Rnd 3: (2 Sc in next sc, sc in next sc) around: 18 sc.

Rnd 4: (2 Sc in next sc, sc in next 2 sc) around: 24 sc.

Rnd 5: (2 Sc in next sc, sc in next 3 sc) around: 30 sc.

Rnd 6: (2 Sc in next sc, sc in next 4 sc) around: 36 sc.

Rnd 7: (2 Sc in next sc, sc in next 5 sc) around: 42 sc.

Rnd 8: (2 Sc in next sc, sc in next 6 sc) around: 48 sc.

Rnd 9: (2 Sc in next sc, sc in next 7 sc) around: 54 sc.

Rnd 10: (2 Sc in next sc, sc in next 8 sc) around: 60 sc.

Rnd 11: (2 Sc in next sc, sc in next 9 sc) around: 66 sc.

Rnd 12: (2 Sc in next sc, sc in next 10 sc) around; slip st in next sc, finish off.

aloe vera plant

TALL SPIKE

Rnd 1 (Right side)**:** With Fern, make an adjustable loop to form a ring, work 3 sc in ring; do **not** join, place marker to indicate beginning of rnd.

Note: Mark Rnd 1 as **right** side.

Rnd 2: Sc in each sc around.

Rnd 3: 2 Sc in each sc around: 6 sc.

Rnd 4: Sc in each sc around.

Rnd 5: (2 Sc in next sc, sc in next sc) around: 9 sc.

Stuff lightly with polyester fiberfill as you work.

Rnd 6: Sc in each sc around.

Rnd 7: (2 Sc in next sc, sc in next 2 sc) around: 12 sc.

Rnds 8–24: Sc in each sc around.

Rnd 25: Sc2tog around; slip st in next sc, finish off leaving a long end for sewing.

MEDIUM SPIKE (Make 2)

Rnd 1 (Right side)**:** With Fern, make an adjustable loop to form a ring, work 3 sc in ring; do **not** join, place marker to indicate beginning of rnd.

Note: Mark Rnd 1 as **right** side.

Rnd 2: Sc in each sc around.

Rnd 3: 2 Sc in each sc around: 6 sc.

Rnd 4: Sc in each sc around.

Rnd 5: (2 Sc in next sc, sc in next sc) around: 9 sc.

Rnd 6: Sc in each sc around.

Rnd 7: (2 Sc in next sc, sc in next 2 sc) around: 12 sc.

Stuff lightly with polyester fiberfill as you work.

Rnds 8–17: Sc in each sc around.

Rnd 18: Sc2tog around; slip st in next sc, finish off leaving a long end for sewing.

SHORT SPIKE (Make 2)

Rnd 1 (Right side)**:** With Fern, make an adjustable loop to form a ring, work 3 sc in ring; do **not** join, place marker to indicate beginning of rnd.

Note: Mark Rnd 1 as **right** side.

Rnd 2: Sc in each sc around.

Rnd 3: 2 Sc in each sc around: 6 sc.

Rnd 4: Sc in each sc around.

Rnd 5: (2 Sc in next sc, sc in next sc) around: 9 sc.

Stuff lightly with polyester fiberfill as you work.

Rnds 6–13: Sc in each sc around.

Rnd 14: (Sc2tog, sc in next sc) around; slip st in next sc, finish off leaving a long end for sewing.

spiral succulent

With Sage, ch 31.

Row 1: 2 Sc in second ch from hook and in each ch across: 60 sc.

Row 2: Ch 1, turn; (sc, dc) in first sc, ch 4, (dc, sc) in next sc, slip st in next sc, ★ (sc, dc) in next sc, ch 4, (dc, sc) in next sc, slip st in next sc; repeat from ★ across; finish off leaving a long end for sewing.

round cactus

With Kelly Green, ch 9.

Row 1 (Wrong side)**:** Sc in second ch from hook, hdc in next 6 chs, sc in last ch: 8 sts.

Note: Mark the **back** of any stitch on Row 1 as **right** side.

Rows 2-15: Turn; working in back loops only *(Fig. 2, page 15)*, sc in first sc, hdc in next 6 hdc, sc in last sc.

Finish off leaving a long end for sewing.

FLOWER

With Yellow, ch 6.

Rnd 1 (Right side)**:** Slip st in sixth ch from hook, (ch 5, slip st in same ch as first slip st) 4 times; finish off leaving a long end for sewing.

Note: Mark Rnd 1 as **right** side.

strings of pearls

LONG STRAND (Make 2)

With Sweet Pea, ch 3.

Row 1: 8 Hdc in third ch from hook, slip st in first hdc to form first pearl, ★ ch 8, 8 hdc in third ch from hook, slip st in first hdc to form next pearl; repeat from ★ 2 times **more**, ch 5; finish off leaving a long end for sewing.

SHORT STRAND (Make 2)

With Sweet Pea, ch 3.

Row 1: 8 Hdc in third ch from hook, slip st in first hdc to form first pearl, ★ ch 8, 8 hdc in third ch from hook, slip st in first hdc to form next pearl; repeat from ★ once **more**, ch 5; finish off leaving a long end for sewing.

finishing

Optional: Fill Planter with approximately 1" (2.5 cm) of plastic poly pellets.

Stuff Planter with polyester fiberfill to within ½" (12 mm) of top edge.

With **wrong** sides of Soil and Planter together and using grey thread and sewing needle, sew Soil in place.

Thread yarn needle with long end on Round Cactus, weave needle through ends of rows, pull tightly to gather top. Secure end; do **not** cut yarn. With **wrong** side together and matching free loops of beginning ch *(Fig. 3, page 15)* to sts on Row 15, whipstitch together using same end *(Fig. 5, page 15)*. Secure end; do **not** cut yarn.

Stuff Round Cactus firmly with polyester fiberfill.

Using same end, sew Round Cactus to Soil.

Using photos as guides for placement and using long ends, sew Spiral Succulent, Aloe Vera Spikes, and Strings of Pearls to Soil. Sew Flower to Round Cactus.

hanger

Rnd 1 (Right side): With White, make an adjustable loop to form a ring, work 8 sc in ring; do **not** join, place marker to indicate beginning of rnd.

Note: Mark Rnd 1 as **right** side.

Rnd 2: 2 Hdc in each sc around: 16 hdc.

Rnd 3: ★ Ch 2, skip next hdc, 2 hdc in next hdc; repeat from ★ around: 16 hdc and 8 ch-2 sps.

Rnd 4: (Ch 2, 2 hdc) twice in each ch-2 sp around: 32 hdc and 16 ch-2 sps.

Rnd 5: (Ch 2, 2 hdc in next ch-2 sp) around.

Rnd 6: (Ch 2, 3 hdc in next ch-2 sp) around: 48 hdc and 16 ch-2 sps.

Rnd 7: (Ch 3, slip st in next ch-2 sp) around: 16 slip sts and 16 ch-3 sps.

Rnds 8 and 9: (Ch 6, slip st in next sp) around.

Rnd 10: 5 Sc in each ch-6 sp around; slip st in next sc, finish off: 80 sc.

First Loop: With **right** side facing, join White with slip st in center sc of any 5-sc group; ch 12, skip next 9 sc, slip st in next sc (center sc); finish off.

Second Loop: With **right** side facing, skip next 9 sc from First Loop and join White with slip st in next sc, ch 12, skip next 9 sc, slip st in next sc (center sc); finish off.

Third and Fourth Loops: With **right** side facing, skip next 9 sc from last Loop made and join White with slip st in next sc, ch 12, skip next 9 sc, slip st in next sc (center sc); finish off.

Cut four 24" (61 cm) strands of White. Secure one end to the center of one Loop. Repeat with remaining 3 strands.

Gather all strands and tie an overhand knot 1" (2.5 cm) from end.

tassel

Cut a piece of cardboard 4" square (10 cm).
Wind White yarn around the cardboard
approximately 9 times. Cut an 18" (45.5 cm)
length of White yarn and insert it under all
the strands at the top of the cardboard;
pull up **tightly** and tie securely. Leave the
yarn ends long enough to attach the tassel.
Cut the yarn at the opposite end of the
cardboard and then remove it *(Fig. A)*. Cut a
16" (40.5 cm) length of White yarn and wrap
it **tightly** around the tassel several times, ¾"
(19 mm) below the top *(Fig. B)*; tie securely.
Trim the ends.

With **right** side of Hanger facing, attach
tassel to center of Rnd 1.

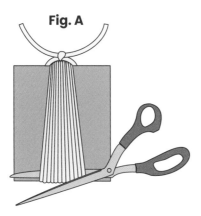

Fig. A

Fig. B

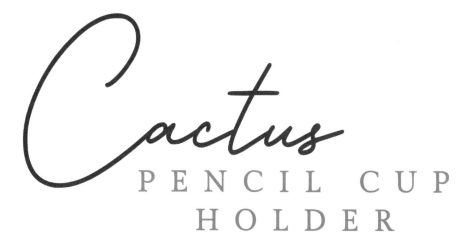

Cactus
PENCIL CUP HOLDER

Add a little pizazz to your work desk with this anything-but-prickly companion. It also doubles as a cute mug cozy for handle-free mugs and cups—just don't try to pick it up by the pom-pom!

Yarn **(Medium Weight)**

(7 ounces, 364 yards [198 grams, 333 meters] per skein):
- Green: 1 skein
- Pink: 20 yards (18.5 meters)

Crochet Hooks

- Size G (4 mm) **and**
- Size H (5 mm)
  or sizes needed for gauge

Additional Supplies

- Yarn needle
- Polyester fiberfill

Gauge Information

Bottom = 3½" (9 cm) diameter

Make a gauge swatch that is 2" (5 cm) diameter. Work same as Bottom for 3 rnds: 18 sc.

Stitch Guide

SINGLE CROCHET 3 TOGETHER *(abbreviated sc3tog)*
Pull up a loop in each of next 3 sc, YO and draw through all 4 loops on hook **(counts as one sc)**.

 **EASY**

Finished Size: 4" bottom diameter x 4¾" tall (10 cm x 12 cm)

side

With larger-size hook and two strands of Green held together, ch 16.

Row 1 (Right side)**:** Sc in second ch from hook and in each ch across: 15 sc.

Note: Mark Row 1 as **right** side.

Rows 2–36: Ch 1, turn; sc in back loop only of each sc across *(Fig. 2, page 15)*.

Finish off leaving long ends for sewing.

Thread yarn needle with long end. With **wrong** side together, working in both loops of sc on Row 36 and in free loops of beginning ch *(Fig. 3, page 15)*, whipstitch piece together *(Fig. 5, page 15)* to form a tube.

Trim: With **right** side facing and larger-size hook, join two strands of Green with sc in end of any row *(see Joining with Sc, page 14)*; sc in end of each row around; join with slip st to first sc, finish off.

Joining Rnd: Place **wrong** sides of Side and Bottom together with Side facing. With larger-size hook and working through ends of rows on Side and in front loops only of sc on Bottom Trim *(Fig. 2, page 15)*, join two strands of Green with sc in any st; sc in each st around; join with slip st to first sc, finish off.

bottom

Rnd 1 (Right side)**:** With larger-size hook and two strands of Green held together, ch 2, 6 sc in second ch from hook; do **not** join, place marker to indicate beginning of rnd *(see Markers, page 14)*.

Note: Loop a short piece of yarn around any stitch to mark Rnd 1 as **right** side.

Rnd 2: 2 Sc in each sc around: 12 sc.

Rnd 3: (Sc in next sc, 2 sc in next sc) around: 18 sc.

Rnd 4: (Sc in next 2 sc, 2 sc in next sc) around: 24 sc.

Rnd 5: (Sc in next 3 sc, 2 sc in next sc) around: 30 sc.

Rnd 6: (Sc in next 4 sc, 2 sc in next sc) around; slip st in next sc, finish off: 36 sc.

arm

With smaller-size hook and one strand of Green, ch 9.

Row 1 (Right side)**:** Sc in second ch from hook and in next ch, 3 sc in next ch, sc in last 5 chs: 10 sc.

Note: Mark Row 1 as **right** side.

Row 2: Ch 1, turn; working in back loops only, sc in first 6 sc, 3 sc in next sc, sc in last 3 sc: 12 sc.

Row 3: Ch 1, turn; working in back loops only, sc in first 4 sc, 3 sc in next sc, sc in last 7 sc: 14 sc.

Row 4: Ch 1, turn; working in back loops only, sc in first 8 sc, 3 sc in next sc, sc in last 5 sc: 16 sc.

Row 5: Ch 1, turn; working in back loops only, sc in first 5 sc, sc3tog, sc in last 8 sc: 14 sc.

Row 6: Ch 1, turn; working in back loops only, sc in first 7 sc, sc3tog, sc in last 4 sc: 12 sc.

Row 7: Ch 1, turn; working in back loops only, sc in first 3 sc, sc3tog, sc in last 6 sc: 10 sc.

Row 8: Ch 1, turn; working in back loops only, sc in first 5 sc, sc3tog, sc in last 2 sc; finish off leaving a long end for sewing: 8 sc.

Thread yarn needle with long end, weave needle through ends of rows, pull tightly to gather top of Arm. Secure end; do **not** cut yarn. With **wrong** side together, working in both loops of sc on Row 8 and in free loops of beginning ch, whipstitch piece together using same end; do **not** cut yarn.

Using photo as a guide for placement and using same end, sew Arm to Side, stuffing firmly with polyester fiberfill before closing.

pom-pom

Cut a piece of cardboard 1" wide x 2" long (2.5 cm x 5 cm).

Wind Pink around the cardboard lengthwise until it is approximately ½" (12 mm) thick in the middle *(Fig. A)*.

Carefully slip the yarn off the cardboard and firmly tie an 18" (45.5 cm) length of yarn around the middle *(Fig. B)*. Leave yarn ends long enough to attach the pom-pom. Cut the loops on both ends and trim the pom-pom into a smooth ball *(Fig. C)*.

Attach pom-pom to top of Arm.

Fig. A

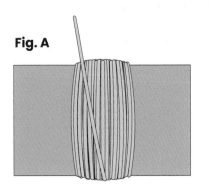

Fig. B

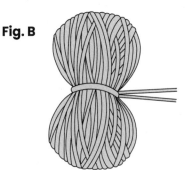

Fig. C

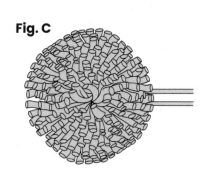

Potholder

This is one cactus you won't mind putting your hands on—or in, as the case may be! It's a fun kitchen accessory that looks cute hanging up while not in use. Before using it for the first time, test how heat-resistant it is by touching a hot item without actually picking it up.

Yarn (Medium Weight)

(2.5 ounces, 120 yards [70.9 grams, 109 meters] per skein):
- Green: 1 skein
- Grey: 1 skein
- White: 5 yards (4.5 meters)
- Peach: small amount

Crochet Hook

- Size G (4 mm)

Additional Supplies

- Yarn needle

Gauge Information

Gauge is not of great importance; your Potholder may be a little larger or smaller without changing the overall effect.

Stitch Guide

HALF DOUBLE CROCHET 2 TOGETHER (*abbreviated hdc2tog*)
   (uses next 2 hdc)
★ YO, insert hook in **next** hdc, YO and pull up a loop; repeat from ★ once **more**, YO and draw through all 5 loops on hook (**counts as one hdc**).

 **INTERMEDIATE**

Finished Size: Approximately 6½" wide x 8½" long (16.5 cm x 21.5 cm)

cactus (Make 2)

With Green, ch 12.

Row 1 (Right side)**:** Sc in second ch from hook and in each ch across to last ch, 4 sc in last ch; working in free loops of beginning ch *(Fig. 3, page 15)*, sc in next 10 chs: 24 sc.

Note: Loop a short piece of yarn around any stitch to mark Row 1 as **right** side.

Row 2: Ch 1, turn; sc in first 2 sc, hdc in next 8 sc, 2 sc in each of next 4 sc, hdc in next 8 sc, sc in last 2 sc: 28 sts.

Row 3: Ch 1, turn; working in back loops only *(Fig. 2, page 15)*, sc in first 2 sc, hdc in next 8 hdc, (2 sc in next sc, sc in next sc) 4 times, hdc in next 8 hdc, sc in last 2 sc: 32 sts.

Row 4: Ch 1, turn; working in both loops, sc in first 2 sc, hdc in next 8 hdc, (2 sc in next sc, sc in next 2 sc) 4 times, hdc in next 8 hdc, sc in last 2 sc: 36 sts.

Row 5: Ch 1, turn; working in back loops only, sc in first 2 sc, hdc in next 8 hdc, 2 hdc in next sc, (hdc in next 3 sc, 2 hdc in next sc) 3 times, hdc in next 11 hdc, sc in last 2 sc: 40 sts.

Row 6: Ch 1, turn; working in both loops, sc in first 2 sc, hdc in next 8 hdc, 2 hdc in next hdc, (hdc in next 4 hdc, 2 hdc in next hdc) 3 times, hdc in next 12 hdc, sc in last 2 sc: 44 sts.

Row 7: Ch 1, turn; working in back loops only, sc in first 2 sc, hdc in next 8 hdc, 2 hdc in next hdc, (hdc in next 5 hdc, 2 hdc in next hdc) 3 times, hdc in next 13 hdc, sc in last 2 sc: 48 sts.

Row 8: Ch 1, turn; working in both loops, sc in first 2 sc, hdc in next 8 hdc, (2 sc in next hdc, sc in next 6 hdc) 4 times, hdc in next 8 hdc, sc in last 2 sc; finish off: 52 sts.

Using photo as a guide for placement and using White, add straight stitch (*Fig. 4, page 15*) "V" shapes to one Cactus (front) as desired.

Joining Row: With **wrong** sides together and matching sts, working through **both** loops of **both** pieces, and having front facing, join Green with sc in first sc (*see Joining with Sc, page 14*); sc in each st across; finish off.

Hanger: With front facing and working behind top of sts on Joining Row, join Green with slip st around center top sc; ch 10; join with slip st to joining slip st, finish off.

planter (Make 2)

With Grey, ch 24.

Row 1 (Right side)**:** Hdc in third ch from hook and in each ch across: 22 hdc.

Note: Mark Row 1 as **right** side.

Rows 2–7: Ch 2 (does **not** count as a st), turn; hdc2tog, hdc in next hdc and in each hdc across: 16 hdc.

Finish off.

Joining Row: With **wrong** sides together and working in ends of rows on both pieces, join Grey with sc in first row; work 10 sc evenly spaced across; working in **both** loops of **both** pieces across Row 7, 3 sc in first hdc, sc in each hdc across to last hdc; 3 sc in last hdc, work 11 sc evenly spaced across ends of rows; finish off leaving a long end for sewing.

flower

With Peach, ch 6.

Rnd 1 (Right side)**:** Slip st in sixth ch from hook, (ch 5, slip st in same ch as first slip st) 4 times; finish off leaving a long end for sewing.

Note: Mark Rnd 1 as **right** side.

finishing

Using photo as a guide for placement and using long ends, place bottom edge of Cactus into top edge of Planter, then sew Planter to Cactus. Sew Flower to front of Cactus.

Prickly Pear
CACTUS

Add a pop of evergreen color to any room with this sturdy little friend. Feel free to adjust the color of the pot or even the flower to suit its intended new home.

Yarn (Medium Weight)

(3.5 ounces, 170 yards [100 grams, 156 meters] per skein):

- Green: 1 skein
- Navy: 1 skein
- Brown: 25 yards (23 meters)
- Light Green: 5 yards (4.5 meters)
- Yellow: small amount

Crochet Hook

- Size G (4 mm) **or** size needed for gauge

Additional Supplies

- Yarn needle
- Sewing needle and dark blue thread
- Polyester fiberfill
- Plastic poly pellets (optional)

Gauge Information

Make a gauge swatch that is 3" (7.5 cm) diameter. Work same as Planter Bottom: 42 sc.

Stitch Guide

SINGLE CROCHET 2 TOGETHER *(abbreviated sc2tog)*
Pull up a loop in each of next 2 sc, YO and draw through all 3 loops on hook **(counts as one sc)**.

 **EASY**

Finished Size: 10½" (26.5 cm) tall

Rnd 6: (Sc in next 4 sc, 2 sc in next sc) around; do **not** finish off: 42 sc.

SIDES

Rnd 1: Sc in back loop only of each sc around (*Fig. 2, page 15*).

Rnds 2–14: Sc in both loops of each sc around; at end of Rnd 14, slip st in next sc, finish off.

soil

Rnd 1 (Right side)**:** With Brown, make an adjustable loop to form a ring, work 6 sc in ring; do **not** join, place marker to indicate beginning of rnd.

Note: Mark Rnd 1 as **right** side.

Rnd 2: 2 Sc in each sc around: 12 sc.

Rnd 3: (Sc in next sc, 2 sc in next sc) around: 18 sc.

Rnd 4: (Sc in next 2 sc, 2 sc in next sc) around: 24 sc.

Rnd 5: (Sc in next 3 sc, 2 sc in next sc) around: 30 sc.

Rnd 6: (Sc in next 4 sc, 2 sc in next sc) around: 36 sc.

Rnd 7: (Sc in next 5 sc, sc in next 2 sc) around; slip st in next sc, finish off.

planter

BOTTOM

With Navy, make an adjustable loop to form a ring (*Figs. 1a-d, page 14*), work 7 sc in ring; do **not** join, place marker to indicate beginning of rnd (*see Markers, page 14*).

Note: Loop a short piece of yarn around any stitch to mark Rnd 1 as **right** side.

Rnd 2: 2 Sc in each sc around: 14 sc.

Rnd 3: (Sc in next sc, 2 sc in next sc) around: 21 sc.

Rnd 4: (Sc in next 2 sc, 2 sc in next sc) around: 28 sc.

Rnd 5: (Sc in next 3 sc, 2 sc in next sc) around: 35 sc.

cactus

LARGE PAD

Rnd 1 (Right side)**:** With Green, make an adjustable loop to form a ring, work 5 sc in ring; do **not** join, place marker to indicate beginning of rnd.

Note: Mark Rnd 1 as **right** side.

Rnd 2: 2 Sc in each sc around: 10 sc.

Rnd 3: (Sc in next sc, 2 sc in next sc) around: 15 sc.

Rnd 4: (Sc in next 2 sc, 2 sc in next sc) around: 20 sc.

Rnd 5: (Sc in next 3 sc, 2 sc in next sc) around: 25 sc.

Rnd 6: (Sc in next 4 sc, 2 sc in next sc) around: 30 sc.

Rnds 7–13: Sc in each sc around.

Rnd 14: (Sc2tog, sc in next 13 sc) twice: 28 sc.

Rnd 15: (Sc2tog, sc in next 12 sc) twice: 26 sc.

Rnd 16: (Sc2tog, sc in next 11 sc) twice: 24 sc.

Rnd 17: (Sc2tog, sc in next 10 sc) twice: 22 sc.

Rnd 18: (Sc2tog, sc in next 9 sc) twice: 20 sc.

Rnds 19 and 20: Sc in each sc around; at end of Rnd 20, slip st in next sc, finish off leaving a long end for sewing.

MEDIUM PAD

Rnd 1 (Right side)**:** With Green, make an adjustable loop to form a ring, work 5 sc in ring; do **not** join, place marker to indicate beginning of rnd.

Note: Mark Rnd 1 as **right** side.

Rnd 2: 2 Sc in each sc around: 10 sc.

Rnd 3: (Sc in next sc, 2 sc in next sc) around: 15 sc.

Rnd 4: (Sc in next 2 sc, 2 sc in next sc) around: 20 sc.

Rnds 5-9: Sc in each sc around.

Rnd 10: (Sc2tog, sc in next 8 sc) twice: 18 sc.

Rnd 11: (Sc2tog, sc in next 7 sc) twice: 16 sc.

Rnd 12: (Sc2tog, sc in next 6 sc) twice: 14 sc.

Rnd 13: (Sc2tog, sc in next 5 sc) twice: 12 sc.

Rnd 14: Sc in each sc around; slip st in next sc, finish off leaving a long end for sewing.

SMALL PAD (Make 2)

Rnd 1 (Right side)**:** With Green, make an adjustable loop to form a ring, work 5 sc in ring; do **not** join, place marker to indicate beginning of rnd.

Note: Mark Rnd 1 as **right** side.

Rnd 2: 2 Sc in each sc around: 10 sc.

Rnd 3: (Sc in next sc, 2 sc in next sc) around: 15 sc.

Rnds 4-6: Sc in each sc around.

Rnd 7: Sc2tog, sc in next 13 sc: 14 sc.

Rnd 8: (Sc2tog, sc in next 5 sc) twice: 12 sc.

Rnd 9: (Sc2tog, sc in next 4 sc) twice; slip st in next sc, finish off leaving a long end for sewing.

SMALLEST PAD

Rnd 1 (Right side)**:** With Green, make an adjustable loop to form a ring, work 5 sc in ring; do **not** join, place marker to indicate beginning of rnd.

Note: Mark Rnd 1 as **right** side.

Rnd 2: 2 Sc in each sc around: 10 sc.

Rnds 3 and 4: Sc in each sc around.

Rnd 5: (Sc2tog, sc in next 3 sc) twice: 8 sc.

Rnd 6: (Sc2tog, sc in next 2 sc) twice; slip st in next sc, finish off leaving a long end for sewing.

flower

With Yellow, ch 6.

Rnd 1 (Right side)**:** Slip st in sixth ch from hook, (ch 5, slip st in same ch as first slip st) 4 times; finish off leaving a long end for sewing.

Note: Mark Rnd 1 as **right** side.

finishing

Optional: Fill Planter with approximately 1" (2.5 cm) of plastic poly pellets.

Stuff Planter with polyester fiberfill to within ½" (12 mm) of top edge.

With **wrong** sides of Soil and Planter together and using blue thread and sewing needle, sew Soil in place.

Using photo as a guide for placement and using Light Green, add straight stitch *(Fig. 4, page 15)* "V" shapes to Pads as desired.

Stuff Pads lightly with polyester fiberfill so that they are flat.

Using photo as a guide for placement and using long ends, sew Flower to one Small Pad. Sew Medium Pad and Small Pad with Flower to Large Pad. Sew remaining Small Pad and Smallest Pad to Medium Pad. Sew bottom of Large Pad to center of Soil.

Saguaro CACTUS

Bring a piece of the Southwest into your home with this striking creation. It has a strong structure and a bright pop of color in the flower.

Yarn (Medium Weight)

(3.5 ounces, 170 yards
[100 grams, 156 meters]
per skein):
- Green: 1 skein
- Grey: 65 yards (59.5 meters)
- Brown: 35 yards (32 meters)
- Rose: 15 yards (13.5 meters)

Crochet Hook

- Size G (4 mm)
  or size needed for gauge

 **INTERMEDIATE**
Finished Size: 10¼" (26 cm) tall

Additional Supplies

- Yarn needle
- Sewing needle and grey thread
- Polyester fiberfill
- Plastic poly pellets (optional)

Gauge Information

Make a gauge swatch that is 2¼" (5.75 cm) diameter. Work same as Planter for 5 rnds: 30 sc.

Stitch Guide

HALF DOUBLE CROCHET 3 TOGETHER *(abbreviated hdc3tog)*
  (uses next 3 hdc)
★ YO, insert hook in **next** hdc, YO and pull up a loop; repeat from ★ 2 times **more**, YO and draw through all 7 loops on hook (**counts as one hdc**).

planter

Rnd 1 (Right side): With Grey, make an adjustable loop to form a ring *(Figs. 1a-d, page 14)*, work 6 sc in ring; do **not** join, place marker to indicate beginning of rnd *(see Markers, page 14)*.

Note: Loop a short piece of yarn around any stitch to mark Rnd 1 as **right** side.

Rnd 2: 2 Sc in each sc around: 12 sc.

Rnd 3: (2 Sc in next sc, sc in next sc) around: 18 sc.

Rnd 4: (2 Sc in next sc, sc in next 2 sc) around: 24 sc.

Rnd 5: (2 Sc in next sc, sc in next 3 sc) around: 30 sc.

Rnd 6: Sc in back loop only of each sc around *(Fig. 2, page 15)*.

Rnd 7: Sc in both loops of each sc around.

Rnd 8: Sc in next 2 sc, 2 sc in next sc, (sc in next 4 sc, 2 sc in next sc) 5 times, sc in next 2 sc: 36 sc.

Rnd 9: (2 Sc in next sc, sc in next 5 sc) around: 42 sc.

Rnd 10: Sc in next 3 sc, 2 sc in next sc, (sc in next 6 sc, 2 sc in next sc) 5 times, sc in next 3 sc: 48 sc.

Rnd 11: (2 Sc in next sc, sc in next 7 sc) around: 54 sc.

Rnd 12: Sc in next 4 sc, 2 sc in next sc, (sc in next 8 sc, 2 sc in next sc) 5 times, sc in next 4 sc: 60 sc.

Rnd 13: (2 Sc in next sc, sc in next 9 sc) around: 66 sc.

Rnd 14: Sc in next 5 sc, 2 sc in next sc, (sc in next 10 sc, 2 sc in next sc) 5 times, sc in next 5 sc: 72 sc.

Rnd 15: (2 Sc in next sc, sc in next 11 sc) around: 78 sc.

Rnds 16-22: Sc in each sc around; at end of Rnd 22, slip st in next sc, finish off.

soil

Rnd 1 (Right side): With Brown, make an adjustable loop to form a ring, work 6 sc in ring; do **not** join, place marker to indicate beginning of rnd.

Note: Mark Rnd 1 as **right** side.

Rnd 2: 2 Sc in each sc around: 12 sc.

Rnd 3: (2 Sc in next sc, sc in next sc) around: 18 sc.

Rnd 4: (2 Sc in next sc, sc in next 2 sc) around: 24 sc.

Rnd 5: (2 Sc in next sc, sc in next 3 sc) around: 30 sc.

Rnd 6: (2 Sc in next sc, sc in next 4 sc) around: 36 sc.

Rnd 7: (2 Sc in next sc, sc in next 5 sc) around: 42 sc.

Rnd 8: (2 Sc in next sc, sc in next 6 sc) around: 48 sc.

Rnd 9: (2 Sc in next sc, sc in next 7 sc) around: 54 sc.

Rnd 10: (2 Sc in next sc, sc in next 8 sc) around: 60 sc.

Rnd 11: (2 Sc in next sc, sc in next 9 sc) around: 66 sc.

Rnd 12: (2 Sc in next sc, sc in next 10 sc) around: 72 sc.

Rnd 13: (2 Sc in next sc, sc in next 11 sc) around; slip st in next sc, finish off.

large cactus

With Green, ch 41.

Row 1 (Wrong side)**:** Sc in second ch from hook, hdc in next 12 chs, sc in next 3 chs, hdc in next ch and in each ch across: 40 sts.

Note: Mark the **back** of any stitch on Row 1 as **right** side.

Row 2: Ch 2, turn; working in back loops only, hdc in first 24 hdc, sc in next sc, slip st in next sc, sc in next sc, hdc in next 12 hdc, sc in last sc.

Row 3: Turn; working in back loops only, sc in first sc, hdc in next 12 hdc, sc in next 3 sts, hdc in next hdc and in each hdc across.

Rows 4–16: Repeat Rows 2 and 3 six times; then repeat Row 2 once **more**.

Finish off leaving a long end for sewing.

arm

With Green and leaving a long end for sewing, ch 15.

Row 1: Sc in second ch from hook, hdc in next 9 chs, 3 hdc in next ch, hdc in last 3 chs: 16 sts.

Row 2 (Right side)**:** Ch 2, turn; working in back loops only, hdc in first 4 hdc, 3 hdc in next hdc, hdc in next 10 hdc, sc in last sc: 18 sts.

Note: Mark Row 2 as **right** side.

Row 3: Turn; working in back loops only, sc in first sc, hdc in next 11 hdc, 3 hdc in next hdc, hdc in last 5 hdc: 20 sts.

Row 4: Ch 2, turn; working in back loops only, hdc in first 6 hdc, 3 hdc in next hdc, hdc in next 12 hdc, sc in last sc: 22 sts.

Row 5: Turn; working in back loops only, sc in first sc, hdc in next st and in each st across.

Row 6: Ch 2, turn; working in back loops only, hdc in first 6 hdc, hdc3tog, hdc in next 12 hdc, sc in last sc: 20 sts.

Row 7: Turn; working in back loops only, sc in first sc, hdc in next 11 hdc, hdc3tog, hdc in last 5 hdc: 18 sts.

Row 8: Ch 2, turn; working in back loops only, hdc in first 4 hdc, hdc3tog, hdc in next 10 hdc, sc in last sc: 16 sts.

Row 9: Turn; working in back loops only, sc in first sc, hdc in next 9 hdc, hdc3tog, hdc in last 3 hdc; finish off leaving a long end for sewing.

medium cactus

With Green, ch 31.

Row 1 (Wrong side)**:** Sc in second ch from hook, hdc in next 10 chs, sc in next 3 chs, hdc in next ch and in each ch across: 30 sts.

Note: Mark the **back** of any stitch on Row 1 as **right** side.

Row 2: Ch 2, turn; working in back loops only, hdc in first 16 hdc, sc in next sc, slip st in next sc, sc in next sc, hdc in next 10 hdc, sc in last sc.

Row 3: Turn; working in back loops only, sc in first sc, hdc in next 10 hdc, sc in next 3 sts, hdc in last 16 hdc.

Rows 4–10: Repeat Rows 2 and 3 three times; then repeat Row 2 once **more**.

Finish off leaving a long end for sewing.

small cactus

With Green and leaving a long end for sewing, ch 21.

Row 1 (Wrong side)**:** Sc in second ch from hook, hdc in next ch and in each ch across: 20 sts.

Note: Mark the **back** of any stitch on Row 1 as **right** side.

Row 2: Ch 2, turn; working in back loops only, hdc in first hdc and in each hdc across to last sc, sc in last sc.

Row 3: Turn; working in back loops only, sc in first sc, hdc in next hdc and in each hdc across.

Rows 4–9: Repeat Rows 2 and 3 three times.

Finish off leaving a long end for sewing.

flower

With Rose and leaving a long end for sewing, ch 9.

Row 1 (Wrong side)**:** Sc in second ch from hook, hdc in next 6 chs, sc in last ch: 8 sts.

Note: Mark the **back** of any stitch on Row 1 as **right** side.

Rows 2–15: Turn; working in back loops only, sc in first sc, hdc in next 6 hdc, sc in last sc.

Finish off leaving a long end for sewing.

finishing

Optional: Fill Planter with approximately 1" (2.5 cm) of plastic poly pellets.

Stuff Planter with polyester fiberfill to within ½" (12 mm) of top edge.

With **wrong** sides of Soil and Planter together and using grey thread, sew Soil in place.

Thread yarn needle with long end on Large Cactus, weave needle through ends of rows, pull tightly to gather top. Secure end; do **not** cut yarn. With **wrong** side together, working in both loops of sc on Row 16 and in free loops of beginning ch (*Fig. 3, page 15*), whipstitch piece together (*Fig. 5, page 15*) using same end. Secure end; do **not** cut yarn.

Sew Medium Cactus in same manner.

Thread yarn needle with long end of Arm. With **wrong** side together and matching free loops of beginning ch to both loops of sts on Row 9, whipstitch piece together to form a tube. Secure end; do **not** cut yarn. Using same end, weave needle through ends of rows, pull tightly to gather top of Arm and secure end.

Stuff Arm firmly with polyester fiberfill. Using photo as a guide for placement and using beginning end, sew to Large Cactus.

Sew Small Cactus and Flower in same manner. Secure end; do **not** cut yarn.

Stuff Flower firmly with polyester fiberfill. Using photo as a guide for placement and using same end, sew to top of Small Cactus.

Stuff each Cactus firmly with polyester fiberfill. Using photo as a guide for placement and using same ends, sew each Cactus to Soil.

Spiral SUCCULENT

This little succulent set is full of texture. Experiment with combining different shades of green for the two individual plants.

Yarn (Medium Weight)

(3.5 ounces, 170 yards [100 grams, 156 meters] per skein):
- White: 1 skein
- Brown: 25 yards (23 meters)
- Sage: 25 yards (23 meters)
- Green: 15 yards (13.5 meters)

Crochet Hook

- Size G (4 mm)
  or size needed for gauge

Additional Supplies

- Yarn needle
- Sewing needle and white thread
- Polyester fiberfill

Gauge Information

15 sc and 15 rows = 3½" (9 cm)

Make a gauge swatch that is 3½" (9 cm) square. Work same as Planter Bottom: 15 sc.

 **EASY**

Finished Size: 3" (7.5 cm) tall

planter

BOTTOM

With White, ch 16.

Row 1 (Right side)**:** Sc in second ch from hook and in each ch across: 15 sc.

Note: Loop a short piece of yarn around any stitch to mark Row 1 as **right** side.

Rows 2-15: Ch 1, turn; sc in each sc across.

Trim: Ch 1, do **not** turn; sc in end of each row across; sc in free loop of next 15 chs *(Fig. 3, page 15)*; sc in end of each row across; sc in each sc across Row 15; do **not** join, place marker to indicate the beginning of rnd *(see Markers, page 14)*; do **not** finish off: 60 sc.

SIDES

Rnd 1: Sc in back loop only of each sc around *(Fig. 2, page 15)*.

Rnds 2-7: Sc in both loops of each sc around; at end of Rnd 7, slip st in next sc, finish off.

SOIL

With Brown, ch 16.

Row 1 (Right side)**:** Sc in second ch from hook and in each ch across: 15 sc.

Note: Mark Row 1 as **right** side.

Rows 2-15: Ch 1, turn; sc in each sc across.

Finish off.

small spiral

With Green, ch 31.

Row 1: 2 Sc in second ch from hook and in each ch across: 60 sc.

Row 2: Ch 1, turn; (sc, dc) in first sc, ch 2, (dc, sc) in next sc, slip st in next sc, ★ (sc, dc) in next sc, ch 2, (dc, sc) in next sc, slip st in next sc; repeat from ★ across; finish off leaving a long end for sewing.

large spiral

With Sage, ch 31.

Row 1: 2 Sc in second ch from hook and in each ch across: 60 sc.

Row 2: Ch 1, turn; (sc, hdc) in first sc, (hdc, sc) in next sc, slip st in next hdc, ★ (sc, hdc) in next sc, (hdc, sc) in next sc, slip st in next sc; repeat from ★ across: 100 sts.

Row 3: Turn; slip st in first slip st, sc in next sc, 2 hdc in next hdc, ch 2, 2 hdc in next hdc, sc in next sc, ★ slip st in next slip st, sc in next sc, 2 hdc in next hdc, ch 2, 2 hdc in next hdc, sc in next sc; repeat from ★ across; finish off leaving a long end for sewing.

finishing

With **wrong** sides of Soil and Planter together and using white thread and sewing needle, sew Soil to Rnd 6 of Sides, stuffing with polyester fiberfill before closing.

Using photo as a guide for placement, sew Spirals to Soil.

Table RUNNER

Whether you use it as a permanent fixture on a side table or as a prominent feature for a special event, this runner will delight anyone who sees it.

Yarn (Medium Weight)

(3.5 ounces, 170 yards [100 grams, 156 meters] per skein):
- Grey: 3 skeins
- Sweet Pea: 1 skein
- Dusty Green: 1 skein
- Sage: 1 skein
- Olive: 1 skein
- Seaspray Mist: 1 skein
- Fern: 1 skein
- Purple: 1 skein

Crochet Hooks

- Size G (4 mm) **and**
- Size M/N (9 mm)
  or sizes needed for gauge

 **INTERMEDIATE**

Finished Size: 11¼" wide x 66" long (28.5 cm x 167.5 cm)

Additional Supplies

- Yarn needle

Gauge Information

With larger-size hook, (hdc, ch 3) 5 times = 4" (10 cm); 10 hdc and 8 rows = 4" (10 cm)

Make a gauge swatch that is 4" (10 cm).

With larger-size hook and Grey, ch 12.

Row 1: Hdc in third ch from hook and in each ch across: 10 hdc.

Rows 2-8: Ch 2 **(does not count as a st)**, hdc in each hdc across.

Finish off.

table runner

With larger-size hook and Grey, ch 30.

Row 1: Hdc in third ch from hook and in each ch across: 28 hdc.

Row 2 (Right side)**:** Ch 2 **(does not count as a st, now and throughout)**, turn; hdc in first hdc and in each hdc across.

Note: Loop a short piece of yarn around any stitch to mark Row 2 as **right** side.

Row 3: Ch 2, turn; hdc in first 2 hdc, ch 3, ★ skip next hdc, hdc in next hdc, ch 3; repeat from ★ across to last 4 hdc, skip next hdc, hdc in last 3 hdc: 16 hdc and 12 ch-3 sps.

Row 4: Ch 2, turn; hdc in first 2 hdc, (ch 3, hdc in next ch-3 sp) across to last 2 hdc, hdc in last 2 hdc.

Repeat Row 4 until piece measures approximately 64½" (164 cm) from beginning ch, ending by working a **wrong** side row.

Next Row: Ch 2, turn; hdc in first 2 hdc, 2 hdc in each of next 12 ch-3 sps, hdc in last 2 hdc: 28 hdc.

Last 2 Rows: Ch 2, turn; hdc in first hdc and in each hdc across.

Finish off.

large spiral

With smaller-size hook and Sage, ch 62.

Row 1: 2 Hdc in third ch from hook and in each ch across: 120 hdc.

Row 2: Ch 1, turn; (sc, dc) in first hdc, (dc, sc) in next hdc, slip st in next hdc, ★ (sc, dc) in next hdc, (dc, sc) in next hdc, slip st in next hdc; repeat from ★ across; finish off leaving a long end for sewing.

small spiral

(Make 2 **each** with Sage, Fern, Sweet Pea, Olive, Seaspray Mist, Dusty Green, and Purple)

With smaller-size hook and color indicated, ch 31.

Row 1: 2 Sc in second ch from hook and in each ch across: 60 sc.

Row 2: Ch 1, turn; (sc, dc) in first sc, ch 2, (dc, sc) in next sc, slip st in next sc, ★ (sc, dc) in next sc, ch 2, (dc, sc) in next sc, slip st in next sc; repeat from ★ across; finish off leaving a long end for sewing.

large spiky spiral

(Make 1 **each** with Sweet Pea and Dusty Green)

With smaller-size hook and color indicated, ch 16.

Row 1 (Right side)**:** 3 Sc in second ch from hook and in each ch across: 45 sc.

Row 2: Ch 1, turn; sc in first sc, (ch 4, sc in second ch from hook and in next ch, hdc in last ch, sc in next sc on Row 1) 5 times, (ch 5, sc in second ch from hook and in next 2 chs, hdc in last ch, sc in next sc on Row 1) 5 times, (ch 6, sc in second ch from hook and in next 3 chs, hdc in last ch, sc in next sc on Row 1) 10 times, (ch 7, sc in second ch from hook and in next 4 chs, hdc in last ch, sc in next sc on Row 1) 10 times, (ch 8, sc in second ch from hook and in next 5 chs, hdc in last ch, sc in next sc on Row 1) 14 times; finish off leaving a long end for sewing.

small spiky spiral

(Make 1 **each** with Sweet Pea, Olive, Seaspray Mist, and Dusty Green)

With smaller-size hook and color indicated, ch 11.

Row 1 (Right side)**:** 3 Sc in second ch from hook and in each ch across: 30 sc.

Row 2: Ch 1, turn; sc in first sc, (ch 4, sc in second ch from hook and in next ch, hdc in last ch, sc in next sc on Row 1) 5 times, (ch 5, sc in second ch from hook and in next 2 chs, hdc in last ch, sc in next sc on Row 1) 5 times, (ch 6, sc in second ch from hook and in next 3 chs, hdc in last ch, sc in next sc on Row 1) 10 times, (ch 7, sc in second ch from hook and in next 4 chs, hdc in last ch, sc in next sc on Row 1) 9 times; finish off leaving a long end for sewing.

finishing

Using photo as a guide for placement and using long ends, sew Spirals to **right** side of center on Table Runner.

fringe

Cut a piece of cardboard 6½" (16.5 cm) square.

Wind Grey **loosely** and **evenly** around the cardboard 56 times, then cut across one end.

Hold 4 strands of yarn together. Fold in half.

With **wrong** side facing and using a crochet hook, draw the folded end up through first stitch and pull the loose ends through the folded end *(Fig. 6a, page 16)*; draw the knot up tightly *(Fig. 6b, page 16)*. Repeat, spacing evenly across short edges of Table Runner.

Lay flat on a hard surface and trim the ends.

Round
CACTUS

Here's a plump plant for fans of a more rounded look.
You'll be sorely tempted to give this guy a squeeze
whenever you walk by.

Yarn (Medium Weight)

- Rust: 50 yards (45.5 meters)
- Green: 30 yards (27.5 meters)
- Brown: 25 yards (23 meters)
- Rose: 10 yards (9 meters)

Crochet Hook

- Size G (4 mm)
  or size needed for gauge

Additional Supplies

- Yarn needle
- Sewing needle and orange thread
- Polyester fiberfill
- Plastic poly pellets (optional)

Gauge Information

Make a gauge swatch that is 2½"
(6.35 cm) diameter. Work same as
Planter for 5 rnds: 30 sc.

 **EASY**

Finished Size: 4" (10 cm) tall

planter

Rnd 1 (Right side): With Rust, make an adjustable loop to form a ring (*Figs. 1a-d, page 14*), work 6 sc in ring; do **not** join, place marker to indicate beginning of rnd (*see Markers, page 14*).

Note: Loop a short piece of yarn around any stitch to mark Rnd 1 as **right** side.

Rnd 2: 2 Sc in each sc around: 12 sc.

Rnd 3: (Sc in next sc, 2 sc in next sc) around: 18 sc.

Rnd 4: (Sc in next 2 sc, 2 sc in next sc) around: 24 sc.

Rnd 5: (Sc in next 3 sc, 2 sc in next sc) around: 30 sc.

Rnd 6: Sc in back loop only of each sc around (*Fig. 2, page 15*).

Rnd 7: (2 Sc in next sc, sc in next 9 sc) around: 33 sc.

Rnds 8 and 9: Sc in each sc around.

Rnd 10: (2 Sc in next sc, sc in next 10 sc) around: 36 sc.

Rnds 11 and 12: Sc in each sc around.

Rnd 13: Working front loops only, (2 sc in next sc, sc in next 5 sc) around: 42 sc.

Rnd 14: Working back loops only, sc in each sc around; slip st in next sc, finish off.

soil

Rnd 1 (Right side): With Brown, make an adjustable loop to form a ring, work 6 sc in ring; do **not** join, place marker to indicate beginning of rnd.

Note: Mark Rnd 1 as **right** side.

Rnd 2: 2 Sc in each sc around: 12 sc.

Rnd 3: (2 Sc in next sc, sc in next sc) around: 18 sc.

Rnd 4: (2 Sc in next sc, sc in next 2 sc) around: 24 sc.

Rnd 5: (2 Sc in next sc, sc in next 3 sc) around: 30 sc.

Rnd 6: (2 Sc in next sc, sc in next 4 sc) around; slip st in next sc, finish off: 36 sc.

cactus

With Green, ch 12.

Row 1 (Wrong side): Sc in second ch from hook, hdc in next 9 chs, sc in last ch: 11 sts.

Note: Mark the **back** of any stitch on Row 1 as **right** side.

Rows 2-17: Turn; working in back loops only, sc in first sc, hdc in next 9 hdc, sc in last sc.

Finish off leaving a long end for sewing.

flower

With Rose, ch 6.

Rnd 1 (Right side)**:** Slip st in fifth ch from hook, ★ ch 5, slip st in same ch as first slip st; repeat from ★ 3 times **more**; finish off leaving a long end for sewing.

Note: Mark Rnd 1 as **right** side.

finishing

Optional: Fill Planter with approximately 1" (2.5 cm) of plastic poly pellets.

Stuff Planter with polyester fiberfill to within ½" (12 mm) of top edge.

With **wrong** sides of Soil and Planter together and using orange thread and sewing needle, sew Soil in place.

Thread yarn needle with long end on Cactus, weave needle through ends of rows, and pull tightly to gather top. Secure end; do **not** cut yarn. With **wrong** side together, working in both loops of sc on Row 17 and in free loops of beginning ch *(Fig. 3, page 15)*, whipstitch piece together *(Fig. 5, page 15)* using same end. Secure end; do **not** cut yarn.

Stuff Cactus firmly with polyester fiberfill. With same end, sew Cactus to center of Soil.

Using photo as a guide for placement and using long end, sew Flower to Cactus.

Succulent
S C R U B B E R

You won't mind soaping up with this sweet scrubber. Its chunky and flexible shape will allow you to get whatever you're scrubbing thoroughly clean.

Yarn (Medium Weight)

- Variegated: 30 yards (27.5 meters)
- Grey: 30 yards (27.5 meters)

Crochet Hook

- Size G (4 mm)

Additional Supplies

- Yarn needle

Gauge Information

Gauge is not of great importance; your Scrubber may be a little larger or smaller without changing the overall effect.

 **EASY**

Finished Size: Approximately 4" (10 cm) diameter

planter

Rnd 1 (Right side)**:** With Grey, make an adjustable loop to form a ring *(Figs. 1a-d, page 14)*, work 6 sc in ring; do **not** join, place marker to indicate beginning of rnd *(see Markers, page 14)*.

Note: Loop a short piece of yarn around any stitch to mark Rnd 1 as **right** side.

Rnd 2: 2 Sc in each sc around: 12 sc.

Rnd 3: (Sc in next sc, 2 sc in next sc) around: 18 sc.

Rnd 4: (Sc in next 2 sc, 2 sc in next sc) around: 24 sc.

Rnd 5: (Sc in next 3 sc, 2 sc in next sc) around: 30 sc.

Rnd 6: (Sc in next 4 sc, 2 sc in next sc) around: 36 sc.

Rnd 7: (Sc in next 5 sc, sc in next 2 sc) around: 42 sc.

Rnd 8: (Sc in next 6 sc, 2 sc in next sc) around; slip st in next sc, finish off: 48 sc.

Rnd 9: Sc in each sc around; finish off.

Hanger: With **wrong** side facing, join Grey with slip st around any sc on Rnd 7, ch 10; join with slip st in joining slip st, finish off.

succulent

With Variegated, ch 41.

Row 1 (Right side)**:** Hdc in third ch from hook and in each ch across: 39 hdc.

Note: Mark Row 1 as **right** side.

Row 2: Ch 2 **(does not count as a st)**, turn; 2 hdc in each hdc across: 78 hdc.

Row 3: Ch 1, turn; (sc, dc) in first hdc, ch 1, (dc, sc) in next hdc, slip st in next hdc, ★ (sc, dc) in next hdc, ch 1, (dc, sc) in next hdc, slip st in next hdc; repeat from ★ across; finish off leaving a long end for sewing.

Using photo as a guide for placement, allow Succulent to spiral, then tack in place. With **wrong** sides together, sew Succulent to Planter.

BOWL

You'll want to make multiples of these petite bowls! They're great for storing knickknacks, keys, sewing supplies, wrapped candies, and a whole lot of other things besides.

Yarn (Medium Weight)

- Green: 70 yards (64 meters)
- Pink: 5 yards (4.5 meters)
- White: 2 yards (1.75 meters)

Crochet Hook

- Size H (5 mm)

Additional Supplies

- Yarn needle

Gauge Information

Gauge is not of great importance; your Bowl may be a little larger or smaller without changing the overall effect.

Stitch Guide

SINGLE CROCHET 2 TOGETHER *(abbreviated sc2tog)*
Pull up a loop in each of next 2 sc, YO and draw through all 3 loops on hook **(counts as one sc).**

 **EASY**

Finished Size: Approximately 4" diameter x 2" tall (10 cm x 5 cm)

bowl

Rnd 1 (Right side)**:** Holding two strands of Green together, ch 2, 6 sc in second ch from hook; do **not** join, place marker to indicate beginning of rnd *(see Markers, page 14).*

Note: Loop a short piece of yarn around any stitch to mark Rnd 1 as **right** side.

Rnd 2: 2 Sc in each sc around: 12 sc.

Rnd 3: (2 Sc in next sc, sc in next sc) around: 18 sc.

Rnd 4: (2 Sc in next sc, sc in next 2 sc) around: 24 sc.

Rnd 5: (2 Sc in next sc, sc in next 3 sc) around: 30 sc.

Rnd 6: (2 Sc in next sc, sc in next 4 sc) around: 36 sc.

Rnd 7: (2 Sc in next sc, sc in next 5 sc) around: 42 sc.

Rnds 8–11: Sc in each sc around.

Rnd 12: (Sc2tog, sc in next 5 sc) around: 36 sc.

Rnd 13: (Sc2tog, sc in next 4 sc) around; slip st in next sc, finish off.

flower

With one strand of Pink, ch 6.

Rnd 1 (Right side)**:** Slip st in fifth ch from hook, ★ ch 5, slip st in same ch as first slip st; repeat from ★ 3 times **more**; finish off leaving a long end for sewing.

Note: Mark Rnd 1 as **right** side.

accent lines

Using photo as a guide for placement and using running stitch or straight stitch *(Fig. 4, page 15)*, add 3 accent lines equally spaced around.

Sew Flower to edge of Bowl.

2

Fabulous FLOWERS

Flowers are fun, quick, and easy to make. This section of the book is a little different from the Succulents section. First, you'll learn how to make fourteen individual flowers and leaves. These are the building blocks for the projects! You can mix and combine them in many ways.

Once you're ready to make a project, choose from five wall hangings and five fashionable accessories with lots of variations. Make more flowers and leaves to decorate and embellish other projects or items around your home. You can even try using them on some of the Succulent projects from this book!

Flowers
& LEAVES

In this special section, you'll learn how to make fourteen individual flowers and leaves. These are the building blocks for the projects that follow.

Yarn (Medium Weight)

5-Petal Flower
- Flower: 4 yards (3.5 meters)
- Contrasting Color: 12" (30.5 cm)

Billy Buttons
- Buttons: 6 yards (5.5 meters)
- Stems: 2 yards (2 meters)

Ranunculus
- 12 yards (11 meters)

Large Daisy
- White: 15 yards (13.5 meters)
- Gold: 4 yards (3.5 meters)

Small Daisy
- White: 8 yards (7.5 meters)
- Gold: 3 yards (2.5 meters)

Large Rose
- 19 yards (17.5 meters)

Small Rose
- 10 yards (9 meters)

Large Mum
- 26 yards (24 meters)

Medium Mum
- 15 yards (13.5 meters)

Small Mum
- 9 yards (8 meters)

Small Leaf
- 4 yards (3.5 meters)

Large Leaf
- 5 yards (4.5 meters)

Daisy Leaf
- 4 yards (3.5 meters)

Laurel Leaf
- 7 yards (6.5 meters)

Crochet Hook

- Size G (4 mm)
  or size indicated in project

Additional Supplies

- Yarn needle
- Polyester fiberfill for Billy Buttons and Daisy

Gauge Information

Gauge is not of great importance; your Flowers and Leaves may be a little larger or smaller without changing the overall effect.

Stitch Guide

TREBLE CROCHET
(abbreviated tr)
YO twice, insert hook in st indicated, YO and pull up a loop (4 loops on hook), (YO and draw through 2 loops on hook) 3 times.

SINGLE CROCHET 2 TOGETHER
(abbreviated sc2tog)
Pull up a loop in each of next 2 sc, YO and draw through all 3 loops on hook (**counts as one sc**).

 **EASY**

5-petal flower

Rnd 1 (Right side)**:** Make an adjustable loop to form a ring *(Figs. 1a-d, page 14)*, work 10 sc in ring; do **not** join.

Note: Loop a short piece of yarn around any stitch to mark Rnd 1 as **right** side.

Rnd 2: In each sc around work (slip st, ch 3, 2 dc, ch 3, slip st); finish off.

Using photo as a guide and using Contrasting Color, embroider a straight stitch on each petal *(Fig. 4, page 15)*.

billy buttons

BUTTON (Make 2)

Rnd 1 (Right side)**:** Make an adjustable loop to form a ring *(Figs. 1a-d, page 14)*, work 4 sc in ring; do **not** join, place marker to indicate beginning of rnd *(see Markers, page 14)*.

Note: Loop a short piece of yarn around any stitch to mark Rnd 1 as **right** side.

Rnd 2: 2 Sc in each sc around: 8 sc.

Rnd 3: Sc in each sc around.

Stuff Button with polyester fiberfill.

Rnd 4: Sc2tog around; slip st in next st, finish off leaving a long end for sewing: 4 sc.

STEMS

Ch 13.

Row 1: Slip st in second ch from hook and in next 5 chs, ch 4, slip st in second ch from hook and in last 2 chs, slip st in same ch already worked into on main ch and in last 6 chs; finish off.

With long end, sew one Button to the end of each Stem.

ranunculus

BOTTOM PETALS

Rnd 1 (Right side)**:** Make an adjustable loop to form a ring (*Figs. 1a-d, page 14*), work 6 sc in ring; do **not** join, place marker to indicate beginning of rnd (*see Markers, page 14*).

Note: Loop a short piece of yarn around any stitch to mark Rnd 1 as **right** side.

Rnd 2: 2 Sc in each sc around: 12 sc.

Rnd 3: (Sc in next sc, 2 sc in next sc) around: 18 sc.

Rnd 4: ★ (Dc, hdc) in next sc, sc in next sc; repeat from ★ around; slip st in next dc, finish off: 27 sts.

MIDDLE PETALS

Rnds 1 and 2: Work same as Bottom Petals: 12 sc.

Rnd 3: ★ (Dc, hdc) in next sc, (sc, dc) in next sc, (hdc, sc) in next sc; repeat from ★ around; slip st in next dc, finish off: 24 sts.

TOP PETALS

Rnd 1: Work same as Bottom Petals: 6 sc.

Note: Mark Rnd 1 as **right** side.

Rnd 2: (Dc, sc) in each sc around; slip st in next dc, finish off leaving a long end for sewing: 12 sts.

Stack Petals and sew around Rnd 1, working through all three layers.

large daisy

PETALS

Rnd 1 (Right side)**:** With White, make an adjustable loop to form a ring *(Figs. 1a-d, page 14)*, work 6 sc in ring; do **not** join, place marker to indicate beginning of rnd *(see Markers, page 14)*.

Note: Loop a short piece of yarn around any stitch to mark Rnd 1 as **right** side.

Rnd 2: 2 Sc in each sc around: 12 sc.

Rnd 3: (2 Sc in next sc, sc in next sc) around: 18 sc.

Rnd 4: ★ Ch 7; sc in second ch from hook and in next ch, hdc in next 2 chs, sc in last 2 chs, sc in next sc on Rnd 3; repeat from ★ around; slip st in first ch of first petal, finish off: 18 petals.

CENTER

Rnds 1-3: With Gold, work same as Petals: 18 sc.

Rnd 4: Sc in each sc around; slip st in next sc, finish off leaving a long end for sewing.

With long end, sew Center to Rnd 3 of Petals, stuffing with polyester fiberfill before closing.

small daisy

PETALS

Rnd 1 (Right side)**:** With White, make an adjustable loop to form a ring *(Figs. 1a-d, page 14)*, work 6 sc in ring; do not join, place marker to indicate beginning of rnd *(see Markers, page 14)*.

Note: Loop a short piece of yarn around any stitch to mark Rnd 1 as **right** side.

Rnd 2: 2 Sc in each sc around: 12 sc.

Rnd 3: ★ Ch 5; sc in second ch from hook, hdc in next 2 chs, sc in last ch, sc in next sc on Rnd 2; repeat from ★ around; slip st in first ch of first petal, finish off: 12 petals.

CENTER

Rnds 1 and 2: With Gold, work same as Petals: 12 sc.

Rnd 3: Sc in each sc around; slip st in next sc, finish off leaving a long end for sewing.

With long end, sew Center to Rnd 2 of Petals, stuffing with polyester fiberfill before closing.

large rose

Ch 21.

Row 1: 2 Dc in fourth ch from hook and in each of next 5 chs, 2 hdc in each of next 6 chs, 2 sc in each of last 6 chs: 37 sts.

Row 2: Ch 1, turn; (sc, hdc) in first sc, ★ (hdc, sc) in next st, (sc, hdc) in next st; repeat from ★ across to last dc, (hdc, sc) in last dc, leave last st unworked: 72 sts.

Row 3 (Right side)**:** Ch 1, turn; sc in first sc, 2 hdc in each of next 2 hdc, ★ sc in next 2 sc, 2 hdc in each of next 2 hdc; repeat from ★ across to last sc, sc in last sc; finish off leaving a long end for sewing: 108 sts.

With **wrong** side facing and placing the last st worked on Row 3 at the center, allowing the piece to naturally curl, and using long end, sew along beginning ch to hold petals in place.

small rose

Ch 15.

Row 1: 2 Dc in fourth ch from hook and in each of next 3 chs, 2 hdc in each of next 4 chs, 2 sc in each of last 4 chs: 25 sts.

Row 2 (Right side)**:** Ch 1, turn; sc in first sc, (2 hdc in each of next 2 sts, sc in next st) across; finish off leaving a long end for sewing: 41 sts.

With **wrong** side facing and placing the first st worked on Row 2 at the center, allowing the piece to naturally curl and with long end, sew along beginning ch to hold petals in place.

large mum

Ch 49.

Row 1 (Right side): In second ch from hook and in each ch across work (slip st, ch 3, tr, ch 3, slip st); finish off leaving a long end for sewing.

With **wrong** side facing and placing the first st worked on Row 1 at the center, allowing the piece to naturally curl, and using long end, sew along beginning ch to hold petals in place.

medium mum

Ch 37.

Row 1 (Right side): In second ch from hook and in each ch across work (slip st, ch 2, dc, ch 2, slip st); finish off leaving a long end for sewing.

With **wrong** side facing and placing the first st worked on Row 1 at the center, allowing the piece to naturally curl, and using long end, sew along beginning ch to hold petals in place.

small mum

Ch 25.

Row 1 (Right side): (Sc, dc, sc) in second ch from hook and in each ch across; finish off leaving a long end for sewing.

With **wrong** side facing and placing the first st worked on Row 1 at the center, allowing the piece to naturally curl and with long end, sew along beginning ch to hold petals in place.

small leaf

Ch 8.

Rnd 1 (Right side)**:** 3 Dc in fourth ch from hook, dc in next ch, hdc in next ch, sc in next ch, (sc, ch 1, sc) in last ch; working in free loops of beginning ch *(Fig. 3, page 15)*, sc in next ch, hdc in next ch, dc in next ch, 3 dc in next ch; join with slip st to first st; ch 9 (stem), slip st in second ch from hook and in each ch across; finish off.

Note: Loop a short piece of yarn around any stitch to mark Rnd 1 as **right** side.

large leaf

Ch 7.

Rnd 1 (Right side)**:** 2 Sc in second ch from hook, hdc in next 3 chs, sc in next ch, 3 sc in last ch; working in free loops of beginning ch *(Fig. 3, page 15)*, sc in next ch, hdc in next 3 chs, 2 sc in next ch; join with slip st to first sc: 15 sts.

Note: Loop a short piece of yarn around any stitch to mark Rnd 1 as **right** side.

Rnd 2: Ch 1, 2 sc in same st as joining, hdc in next sc, 2 dc in each of next 2 hdc, hdc in next 2 sts, sc in next sc, (sc, ch 2, sc) in next sc, sc in next sc, hdc in next 2 sts, 2 dc in each of next 2 hdc, hdc in next sc, 2 sc in last sc; join with slip st to first sc; ch 11 (stem), slip st in second ch from hook and in each ch across; finish off.

laurel leaf

TOP LEAF & STEM

Rnd 1 (Right side)**:** Ch 4, sc in second ch from hook and in next ch, 4 dc in last ch; working in free loops of beginning ch *(Fig. 3, page 15)*, sc in next 2 chs; join with slip st to first sc; ch 15 (stem), slip st in second ch from hook and in each ch across; finish off.

Note: Loop a short piece of yarn around any stitch to mark Rnd 1 as **right** side.

daisy leaf

Ch 12.

Rnd 1 (Right side)**:** Sc in sixth ch from hook and in next ch, ch 5, (sc in next 2 chs, ch 4) twice, (sc, ch 4) twice in last ch; working in free loops of beginning ch *(Fig. 3, page 15)*, sc in next 2 chs, ch 4, (sc in next 2 chs, ch 5) twice, slip st in next ch; ch 7 (stem), slip st in second ch from hook and in each ch across; finish off.

Note: Loop a short piece of yarn around any stitch to mark Rnd 1 as **right** side.

DOUBLE LEAVES (Make 2)

Ch 10.

Row 1 (Right side)**:** Dc in fourth ch from hook, hdc in next ch, sc in next ch, slip st in next ch, sc in next ch, hdc in next ch, (dc, ch 3, slip st) in last ch; finish off.

Note: Loop a short piece of yarn around any stitch to mark Row 1 as **right** side.

Using photo as a guide for placement, sew Double Leaves to Stem.

Antler
WALL HANGING

If you love a woodsy look but want it to feel softer, this is the perfect project for you. It goes great above a framed picture, a mirror, or a doorway.

Yarn (Medium Weight)

- Linen: 60 yards (55 meters)
- Pink: 19 yards (17.5 meters)
- Grey: 8 yards (7.5 meters)
- Light Blue: 8 yards (7.5 meters)
- Light Olive: 14 yards (13 meters)
- Olive: 5 yards (4.5 meters)
- White: small amount

Crochet Hook

- Size G (4 mm)

Additional Supplies

- Yarn needle
- Strong thread (for hanger)
- Polyester fiberfill

Gauge Information

Gauge is not of great importance; your Flowers and Leaves may be a little larger or smaller. The Antlers need a tight gauge.

Stitch Guide

SINGLE CROCHET 2 TOGETHER *(abbreviated sc2tog)*
Pull up a loop in each of next 2 sc, YO and draw through all 3 loops on hook **(counts as one sc)**.

 **EASY**

Finished Size: 4" x 12" (10 cm x 30.5 cm)

antler (Make 2)

MAIN PIECE

Rnd 1 (Right side)**:** With Linen, make an adjustable loop to form a ring (*Figs. 1a-d, page 14*), work 4 sc in ring; do **not** join, place marker to indicate beginning of rnd (*see Markers, page 14*).

Rnd 2: Sc in each sc around.

Rnd 3 (Increase rnd)**:** 2 Sc in next sc, sc in each sc around: 5 sc.

Rnds 4-6: Repeat Rnds 2 and 3 once, then repeat Rnd 2 once **more**: 6 sc.

Stuff piece with polyester fiberfill as you work.

Rnds 7 and 8: 2 Sc in next sc, sc in next sc, sc2tog, sc in next 2 sc.

Rnds 9 and 10: Sc in each sc around.

Rnd 11: 2 Sc in next sc, sc in each sc around: 7 sc.

Rnds 12 and 13: Sc in each sc around.

Rnd 14: 2 Sc in next sc, sc in each sc around: 8 sc.

Rnds 15-17: Sc in each sc around.

Rnds 18-20: Sc in next 2 sc, 2 sc in next sc, sc in next 3 sc, sc2tog.

Rnds 21-32: Sc in each sc around.

Rnd 33: (2 Sc in next sc, sc in next sc) around: 12 sc.

Rnd 34: Working in back loops only *(Fig. 2, page 15)*, sc2tog around; slip st in next st, finish off leaving a long end for closing: 6 sc.

With long end, sew opening closed.

SHORT PIECE

Rnds 1-8: Work same as Main Piece: 6 sc.

Rnd 9: (2 Sc in next sc, sc in next sc) around; slip st in next st, finish off leaving a long end for sewing: 9 sc.

LONG PIECE

Rnds 1-6: Work same as Main Piece: 6 sc.

Stuff piece with polyester fiberfill as you work.

Rnds 7 and 8: Sc in each sc around.

Rnd 9: Sc in next 4 sc, 2 sc in next sc, sc in next sc: 7 sc.

Rnd 10: Sc in each sc around.

Rnd 11: Sc in next 4 sc, 2 sc in next sc, sc in next 2 sc: 8 sc.

Rnd 12: Sc in each sc around.

Rnd 13: Sc in next 4 sc, 2 sc in next sc, sc in next 3 sc; slip st in next st, finish off leaving a long end for sewing: 9 sc.

Using photo as a guide for placement and using long ends, sew Short and Long Pieces to Main Piece.

base

Rnd 1 (Right side)**:** With Linen, make an adjustable loop to form a ring, work 6 sc in ring; do **not** join, place marker to indicate beginning of rnd.

Note: Loop a short piece of yarn around any stitch to mark Rnd 1 as **right** side.

Rnd 2: 2 Sc in each sc around: 12 sc.

Rnd 3: (2 Sc in next sc, sc in next sc) around: 18 sc.

Rnd 4: (2 Sc in next sc, sc in next 2 sc) around: 24 sc.

Rnd 5: (2 Sc in next sc, sc in next 3 sc) around: 30 sc.

Rnd 6: (2 Sc in next sc, sc in next 4 sc) around; slip st in next sc, finish off leaving a long end for sewing: 36 sc.

Sew both Antlers to Base.

flowers & leaves

With Light Blue, make two 5-Petal Flowers (*page 94*), working straight sts with White.

With Pink, make one Large Rose (*page 97*).

With Grey, make two Small Leaves (*page 99*).

With Olive, make one Large Leaf (*page 99*).

With Light Olive, make two Laurel Leaves (*page 100*).

Using photo as a guide for placement, sew Leaves to Base, then sew one 5-Petal Flower on each side and Large Rose at center.

Using a 10" (25.5 cm) piece of strong thread, sew ends at back of Antlers for hanger.

Wreath

Make a timeless flower wreath that will never fade or wilt! The antler accents and grapevine base add a rustic touch. This project is super customizable—use any collection of flowers and leaves you want.

Yarn (Medium Weight)

- Linen: 55 yards (50.5 meters)
- Light Olive: 42 yards (38.5 meters)
- Pink: 38 yards (34.5 meters)
- Ecru: 28 yards (25.5 meters)
- Rose: 26 yards (24 meters)
- Gold: 18 yards (16.5 meters)
- White: 18 yards (16.5 meters)
- Light Blue: 16 yards (14.5 meters)
- Green: 18 yards (16.5 meters)
- Light Green: 14 yards (13 meters)
- Olive: 10 yards (9 meters)

Crochet Hook

- Size G (4 mm)

Additional Supplies

- Yarn needle
- 14" (35.5 cm) grapevine wreath
- Polyester fiberfill

Gauge Information

Gauge is not of great importance; your Flowers and Leaves may be a little larger or smaller. The Antlers need a tight gauge.

Stitch Guide

SINGLE CROCHET 2 TOGETHER *(abbreviated sc2tog)*
Pull up a loop in each of next 2 sc, YO and draw through all 3 loops on hook **(counts as one sc)**.

 **EASY**

Finished Size: 14" (35.5 cm) diameter

antler (Make 2)

MAIN PIECE

Rnd 1 (Right side): With Linen, make an adjustable loop to form a ring *(Figs. 1a-d, page 14)*, work 4 sc in ring; do **not** join, place marker to indicate beginning of rnd *(see Markers, page 14)*.

Rnd 2: Sc in each sc around.

Rnd 3 (Increase rnd)**:** 2 Sc in next sc, sc in each sc around: 5 sc.

Rnds 4–6: Repeat Rnds 2 and 3 once, then repeat Rnd 2 once **more**: 6 sc.

Stuff piece with polyester fiberfill as you work.

Rnds 7 and 8: 2 Sc in next sc, sc in next sc, sc2tog, sc in next 2 sc.

Rnds 9 and 10: Sc in each sc around.

Rnd 11: 2 Sc in next sc, sc in each sc around: 7 sc.

Rnds 12 and 13: Sc in each sc around.

Rnd 14: 2 Sc in next sc, sc in each sc around: 8 sc.

Rnds 15-17: Sc in each sc around.

Rnds 18-20: Sc in next 2 sc, 2 sc in next sc, sc in next 3 sc, sc2tog.

Rnds 21-32: Sc in each sc around.

Rnd 33: (2 Sc in next sc, sc in next sc) around: 12 sc.

Rnd 34: Working in back loops only (*Fig. 2, page 15*), sc2tog around; slip st in next st, finish off leaving a long end for closing: 6 sc.

With long end, sew opening closed.

SHORT PIECE
Rnds 1-8: Work same as Main Piece: 6 sc.

Rnd 9: (2 Sc in next sc, sc in next sc) around; slip st in next st, finish off leaving a long end for sewing: 9 sc.

LONG PIECE
Rnds 1-6: Work same as Main Piece: 6 sc.

Stuff piece with polyester fiberfill as you work.

Rnds 7 and 8: Sc in each sc around.

Rnd 9: Sc in next 4 sc, 2 sc in next sc, sc in next sc: 7 sc.

Rnd 10: Sc in each sc around.

Rnd 11: Sc in next 4 sc, 2 sc in next sc, sc in next 2 sc: 8 sc.

Rnd 12: Sc in each sc around.

Rnd 13: Sc in next 4 sc, 2 sc in next sc, sc in next 3 sc; slip st in next st, finish off leaving a long end for sewing: 9 sc.

Using photo as a guide for placement and using long ends, sew Short and Long Pieces to Main Piece. Sew both Antlers to wreath.

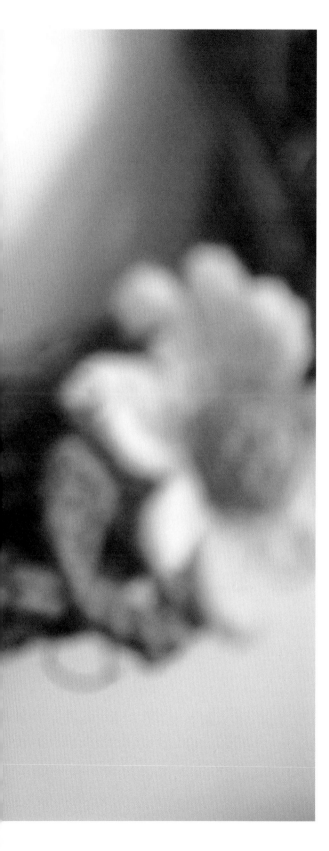

hanger

With Ecru, ch 31.

Row 1: Sc in second ch from hook and in each ch across; finish off.

flowers & leaves

With Light Blue, make four 5-Petal Flowers *(page 94)*, working straight sts with White.

With Gold for Buttons and Light Green for Stems, make two Billy Buttons *(page 94)*.

With Ecru, make two Ranunculus *(page 95)*.

Make two Small Daisies *(page 96)*.

With Pink, make two Large Roses *(page 97)*.

With Rose, make one Large Mum *(page 98)*.

With Green, make two Small Leaves *(page 99)*.

Make six Large Leaves *(page 99)*, two **each** using Light Green, Green, and Olive.

With Light Olive, make six Laurel Leaves *(page 100)*.

Using photo as a guide for placement, sew Flowers and Leaves to wreath.

Sew Hanger to back of wreath.

Garland

This mix of ranunculus flowers and roses combines to make a timeless decoration that can hang on the mantle year-round. Or bring it out for a special event, like a bridal shower or family dinner.

Yarn (Medium Weight)

- Rose: 135 yards (123 meters)
- Off White: 75 yards (68.5 meters)
- Green: 60 yards (55 meters)

Crochet Hook

- Size G (4 mm)

Additional Supplies

- Yarn needle

Gauge Information

Gauge is not of great importance; your Flowers and Leaves may be a little larger or smaller without changing the overall effect.

 **EASY**

Finished Size: 4½ feet (137 cm) long

garland

FIRST END LEAF (Right side)

With Green, ch 4, sc in second ch from hook and in next ch, 4 dc in last ch; working in free loops of beginning ch *(Fig. 3, page 15)*, sc in next 2 chs; join with slip st to first sc: 8 sts.

Note: Loop a short piece of yarn around any stitch to mark Leaf as **right** side.

Chain: Ch 251; sc in second ch from hook and in each ch across; finish off.

SECOND END LEAF

Work same as First End Leaf; finish off leaving a long end for sewing.

With long end, sew Leaf to second end of long chain.

flowers & leaves

With Off White, make six Ranunculus
(*page 95*).

With Rose, make seven Large Roses
(*page 97*).

With Green, make sixteen Double Leaves
(*page 100*).

Using photo as a guide for placement, sew
Flowers and Leaves to chain.

Burlap & FLOWERS

An embroidery hoop makes the perfect base for a modern, classy wall hanging. Customize the arrangement of the flowers however you like—just be sure to create a balanced composition.

Yarn (Medium Weight)

- Light Gold: 26 yards (24 meters)
- Off White: 25 yards (23 meters)
- Green: 19 yards (17.5 meters)
- Dark Green: 18 yards (16.5 meters)
- Rose: 8 yards (7.5 meters)

Crochet Hook

- Size G (4 mm)

Additional Supplies

- Yarn needle
- 8" (20.5 cm) embroidery hoop
- Burlap: 10" (25.5 cm) square
- Fabric glue

Gauge Information

Gauge is not of great importance; your Flowers and Leaves may be a little larger or smaller without changing the overall effect.

 **EASY**

Finished Size: 8" (20.5cm) diameter

flowers & leaves

With Rose, make two 5-Petal Flowers
(page 94), working straight sts with Off White.

With Off White, make two Ranunculus
(page 95).

With Light Gold, make one Large Mum
(page 98).

With Dark Green, make two Small Leaves
(page 99).

With Dark Green, make two Large Leaves
(page 99).

With Green, make one Large Leaf *(page 99)*.

With Green, make two Laurel Leaves
(page 100).

Place the burlap inside the hoop, being sure
to make it taut in the hoop. On the back, trim
the burlap to ½" (12 mm) around. Glue the
burlap to the inside of the hoop.

Using photo as a guide for placement, sew
Flowers and Leaves to burlap.

Dreamcatcher

This nighttime companion makes a great gift. The delicate doily will wow whomever receives it!

Yarn (Medium Weight)

- White: 25 yards (23 meters)
- Light Grey: 20 yards (18.5 meters)
- Pink: 20 yards (18.5 meters)
- Light Rose: 19 yards (17.5 meters)
- Taupe: 18 yards (16.5 meters)
- Light Olive: 14 yards (13 meters)
- Olive: 5 yards (4.5 meters)

Crochet Hook

- Size G (4 mm)
  or size needed for gauge

Additional Supplies

- Yarn needle
- 8" (20.5 cm) embroidery hoop
- Strong white thread
- Straight pins

Gauge Information

Make a gauge swatch that is 2½" (6.25 cm) diameter at points. Work same as Doily through Rnd 2.

 **INTERMEDIATE**

Finished Size: 8" (20.5 cm) diameter ring

doily

Rnd 1 (Right side)**:** With White, ch 6, sc in first ch made, (ch 5, sc in same ch) 4 times, ch 3, hdc in same ch to form last ch-5 sp: 6 ch-5 sps.

Note: Loop a short piece of yarn around any stitch to mark Rnd 1 as **right** side.

Rnd 2: Ch 1, sc in last sp made, ch 5, (sc in next ch-5 sp, ch 5) around; join with slip st to first sc.

Rnd 3: Ch 1, sc in same st as joining, ch 5, sc in next ch-5 sp, ★ ch 5, sc in next sc, ch 5, sc in next ch-5 sp; repeat from ★ around, ch 3, hdc in first sc to form last ch-5 sp: 12 ch-5 sps.

Rnd 4: Ch 1, sc in last sp made, (ch 5, sc in next ch-5 sp) around, ch 3, hdc in first sc to form last ch-5 sp.

Rnd 5: Ch 1, sc in last sp made, ch 6, (sc in next ch-5 sp, ch 6) around; join with slip st to first sc.

Rnd 6: Ch 1, in each ch-6 sp around work (2 sc, hdc, dc, ch 2, dc, hdc, 2 sc); join with slip st to first sc, finish off.

Wind Taupe around the inside piece of the embroidery hoop, covering the entire piece; using yarn needle, secure yarn ends.

Place Doily inside hoop and pin the ch-2 sps on Rnd 6 to the hoop, evenly spaced around; then sew points in place with strong thread. Attach White for hanger.

flowers & leaves

With Light Rose, make one Large Rose *(page 97)*.

With Pink, make two Small Roses *(page 97)*.

With Taupe, make two Small Leaves *(page 99)*.

With Olive, make one Large Leaf *(page 99)*.

With Light Olive, make two Laurel Leaves *(page 100)*.

Using photo as a guide for placement, sew Flowers and Leaves to ring.

fringe

Cut 30 strands of Light Grey, each 22" (56 cm) long. Using photo as a guide for placement and holding 3 strands together, add 10 fringes around hoop *(Figs. 6a & b, page 16)*.

Daisy

Flower Bouquet

Mum

Barrettes

Choose from three designs to make an eye-catching accessory that can easily do double duty as a bag decoration or brooch for your button-down.

Yarn (Medium Weight)

Daisy
- Green: 16 yards (14.5 meters)
- Gold: 9 yards (8 meters)
- White: 8 yards (7.5 meters)
- Light Green: 6 yards (5.5 meters)

Flower Bouquet
- Pink: 19 yards (17.5 meters)
- Light Olive: 14 yards (13 meters)
- Ecru: 10 yards (9 meters)
- Light Blue: 8 yards (7.5 meters)
- Olive: 4 yards (3.5 meters)
- White: small amount

Mum
- Rose: 26 yards (24 meters)
- Light Olive: 14 yards (13 meters)
- Olive: 5 yards (4.5 meters)

Crochet Hook

- Size G (4 mm)

Additional Supplies

- Yarn needle
- Polyester fiberfill (for Daisy Barrette)
- Barrette or clip

Gauge Information

Gauge is not of great importance; your Flowers and Leaves may be a little larger or smaller without changing the overall effect.

 **EASY**

Finished Size: Approximately 4" (10 cm) diameter

base

Rnd 1 (Right side)**:** With Green or Light Olive, make an adjustable loop to form a ring (*Figs. 1a-d, page 14*), work 6 sc in ring; do **not** join, place marker to indicate beginning of rnd (*see Markers, page 14*).

Note: Loop a short piece of yarn around any stitch to mark Rnd 1 as **right** side.

Rnd 2: 2 Sc in each sc around: 12 sc.

Rnd 3: (2 Sc in next sc, sc in next sc) around: 18 sc.

Rnd 4: (2 Sc in next sc, sc in next 2 sc) around: 24 sc.

Rnd 5: (2 Sc in next sc, sc in next 3 sc) around; slip st in next sc, finish off: 30 sc.

Sew barrette or clip to **right** side of Base.

daisy

With Gold for Buttons and Light Green for Stems, make one Billy Buttons (*page 94*).

Make one Small Daisy (*page 96*).

With Light Green, make one Small Leaf (*page 99*).

With Green, make one Large Leaf (*page 99*).

With Green, make one Daisy Leaf (*page 100*).

Using photo as a guide for placement, sew Flowers and Leaves to Base.

flower bouquet

With Light Blue, make two 5-Petal Flowers (*page 94*), working straight sts with White.

With Pink, make one Large Rose (*page 97*).

With Ecru, make one Small Rose (*page 97*).

With Olive, make one Small Leaf (*page 99*).

With Light Olive, make one Laurel Leaf (*page 100*).

Using photo as a guide for placement, sew Flowers and Leaves to Base.

mum

With Rose, make one Large Mum (*page 98*).

With Olive, make one Large Leaf (*page 99*).

With Light Olive, make one Laurel Leaf (*page 100*).

Using photo as a guide for placement, sew Flower and Leaves to Base.

Floral
COWL

Keep warm in chilly weather with this sweet but practical accessory. Choose a yarn whose feel you love on your skin!

Yarn (Medium Weight)

(3 ounces, 197 yards [85 grams, 180 meters] per skein):
- Main Color: 1 skein
- Contrasting Color: 70 yards (64 meters)

Crochet Hook

- Size I (5.5 mm)
  or size needed for gauge

Additional Supplies

- Yarn needle

 **INTERMEDIATE**

Finished Size: 25¾" circumference x 10" wide before folding (65.5 cm x 25.5 cm)

Gauge Information

In pattern, 14 sts and 10 rows = 3¾" (9.5 cm)

Make a gauge swatch that is 4" (10 cm) square.

With Main Color, ch 16.

Row 1: Hdc in second ch from hook, ★ ch 1, skip next ch, hdc in next ch; repeat from ★ across: 15 sts.

Row 2: Ch 1, turn; hdc in first hdc and in next ch-1 sp, (ch 1, hdc in next ch-1 sp) across, hdc in last hdc.

Row 3: Ch 1, turn; hdc in first hdc, ch 1, (hdc in next ch-1 sp, ch 1) across, skip next hdc, hdc in last hdc.

Rows 4-10: Repeat Rows 2 and 3 three times; then repeat Row 2 once **more**.

Finish off.

cowl

With Main Color, ch 96; being careful **not** to twist ch, join with slip st to form a ring.

Rnd 1: Ch 1, hdc in each ch around; join with slip st to first hdc: 96 hdc.

Rnd 2 (Right side)**:** Ch 1, turn; hdc in same st as joining, ch 1, skip next hdc, ★ hdc in next hdc, ch 1, skip next hdc; repeat from ★ around; join with slip st to first hdc: 48 hdc and 48 ch-1 sps.

Note: Loop a short piece of yarn around any stitch to mark Rnd 2 as **right** side.

Rnds 3–23: Ch 1, turn; (hdc in next ch-1 sp, ch 1) around; join with slip st to first hdc.

Rnd 24: Ch 1, turn; 2 hdc in each ch-1 sp around; join with slip st to first hdc, finish off: 96 hdc.

Rnd 25: With **wrong** side facing, join Contrasting Color with sc in same st as joining (*see Joining with Sc, page 14*); ch 2, skip next 2 hdc, ★ sc in next hdc, ch 2, skip next 2 hdc; repeat from ★ around; join with slip st to first sc: 32 sc and 32 ch-2 sps.

Rnd 26: Ch 1, turn; (sc, ch 2) twice in each ch-2 sp around; join with slip st to first sc: 64 sc and 64 ch-2 sps.

Rnd 27: Turn; slip st in first ch-2 sp, (sc, hdc, sc) in next ch-2 sp, ★ slip st in next ch-2 sp, (sc, hdc, sc) in next ch-2 sp; repeat from ★ around; join with slip st to first slip st, finish off.

Fold top 12 rows to **right** side.

flowers & leaf

With Contrasting Color, make: one Ranunculus *(page 95)*, one Small Rose *(page 97)*, and one Small Leaf *(page 99)*.

Using photo as a guide for placement, sew Flowers and Leaf to Cowl.

With Main Color, embroider French knot in center of Ranunculus *(Fig. A)*.

FRENCH KNOT

Bring needle up at 1. Wrap yarn around the needle and insert needle at 2, holding end of yarn with non-stitching fingers *(Fig. A)*. Tighten knot; then pull needle through, holding yarn until it must be released.

Fig. A

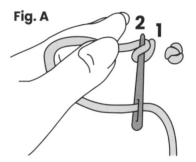

Daisy PURSE

Channel your inner flower child with this design straight from the sixties. It's big enough to be practical but small enough to suit a wide range of outfits.

Yarn (Medium Weight)

(3.5 ounces, 170 yards
[100 grams, 156 meters] per skein):

- Main Color: 2 skeins
- White: 23 yards (21 meters)
- Gold: 13 yards (12 meters)
- Light Green: 10 yards (9 meters)

Crochet Hooks

- Size G (4 mm) **and**
- Size I (5.5 mm)
  or sizes needed for gauge

Additional Supplies

- Yarn needle
- Polyester fiberfill

Gauge Information

With larger-size hook,
12 hdc = 4" (10 cm);
10 rows = 4¼" (10.75 cm)

Make a gauge swatch that is 4" wide x 4¼" high (10 cm x 10.75 cm). With larger-size hook and Main Color, ch 14. Work same as Back for 10 rows; finish off: 12 hdc.

 **EASY**

Finished Size: 10" wide x 12" high
(25.5 cm x 30.5 cm) excluding fringe and strap

back

With larger-size hook and Main Color, ch 32.

Row 1 (Right side)**:** Hdc in third ch from hook and in each ch across: 30 hdc.

Note: Loop a short piece of yarn around any stitch to mark Row 1 as **right** side.

Rows 2-28: Ch 2 **(does not count as a st)**, turn; hdc in each hdc across.

Finish off.

front

Work same as Back; do **not** finish off.

Joining: Holding pieces with **wrong** sides together and working through **both** pieces, sc evenly across end of rows; working in free loops of beginning chs *(Fig. 3, page 15)*, 3 sc in first ch, sc in each ch across to last ch, 3 sc in last ch; sc evenly across end of rows; slip st in next st, finish off.

shoulder strap

With larger-size hook and Main Color, ch 142.

Rows 1 and 2: Work same as Back: 140 hdc.

Finish off leaving a long end for sewing.

Sew Strap to top edge of Front and Back at sides.

fringe

Cut 42 strands of Main Color, each 15" (38 cm) long. Holding 6 strands together, add fringe at each bottom corner and 5 more evenly spaced across *(Figs. 6a & b, page 16)*.

flowers & leaves

Use smaller-size hook for all Flowers and Leaves.

With Gold for Buttons and Light Green for Stems, make one Billy Buttons *(page 94)*.

Make one Large Daisy *(page 96)*.

Make one Small Daisy *(page 96)*.

With Light Green, make two Daisy Leaves *(page 100)*.

Using photo as a guide for placement, sew Flowers and Leaves to Front.

Drawstring PURSE

If you want to make a statement with something small but stunning, this bouquet purse is the way to go. It will only fit the essentials, but you'll be delighted each time you open it up.

Yarn (Medium Weight)

- Green: 70 yards (64 meters)
- Taupe: 60 yards (55 meters)
- Rose: 30 yards (27.5 meters)
- White: 25 yards (23 meters)
- Aqua: 12 yards (11 meters)
- Yellow: 9 yards (8 meters)

Crochet Hook

- Size G (4 mm)
  or size needed for gauge

Additional Supplies

- Yarn needle
- Polyester fiberfill

Gauge Information

Make a gauge swatch that is 2½" (6.5 cm) diameter. Work same as Bottom.

 **INTERMEDIATE**

Finished Size: 2½" diameter at bottom x 6" high (6.5 cm x 15 cm)

bottom

Rnd 1 (Right side): With Taupe, make an adjustable loop to form a ring (*Figs. 1a-d, page 14*), work 6 sc in ring; do **not** join, place marker to indicate beginning of rnd (*see Markers, page 14*).

Note: Loop a short piece of yarn around any stitch to mark Rnd 1 as **right** side.

Rnd 2: 2 Sc in each sc around: 12 sc.

Rnd 3: (2 Sc in next sc, sc in next sc) around: 18 sc.

Rnd 4: (2 Sc in next sc, sc in next 2 sc) around: 24 sc.

Rnd 5: (2 Sc in next sc, sc in next 3 sc) around: 30 sc.

Rnd 6: (2 Sc in next sc, sc in next 4 sc) around: 36 sc.

sides

Rnd 1: Working in back loops only (*Fig. 2, page 15*), sc in each sc around.

Rnd 2: Working in both loops, (2 sc in next sc, sc in next 11 sc) around: 39 sc.

Rnd 3: Sc in each sc around.

Rnd 4: (2 Sc in next sc, sc in next 12 sc) around: 42 sc.

Rnd 5: Sc in each sc around.

Rnd 6: (2 Sc in next sc, sc in next 13 sc) around: 45 sc.

Rnd 7: Sc in each sc around.

Rnd 8: (2 Sc in next sc, sc in next 14 sc) around: 48 sc.

Rnd 9: Sc in each sc around.

Rnd 10: Working in front loops only, (2 sc in next sc, sc in next 7 sc) around; slip st in next sc, finish off: 54 sc.

Rnd 11: With **right** side facing and working in free loops only of Rnd 9 (*Fig. A*), join Green with slip st in same st as joining; sc in same st and in each sc around, place marker to indicate beginning of rnd: 48 sc.

Fig. A

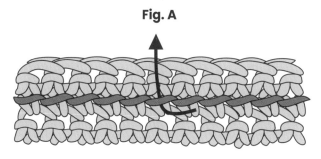

Rnd 12: (2 Hdc in next sc, hdc in next 7 sc) around: 54 hdc.

Rnds 13–21: Hdc in each hdc around.

Rnd 22 (Eyelet rnd)**:** Hdc in next 3 hdc, ch 1, skip next hdc, (hdc in next 5 hdc, ch 1, skip next hdc) 8 times, sc in next 2 hdc; slip st in next hdc, finish off: 50 hdc and 10 ch-1 sps.

drawstring

With Green, ch 80; finish off.

Weave Drawstring through ch-1 sps on Eyelet rnd; tie ends together and trim to 1" (2.5 cm).

flowers

With Aqua, make three 5-Petal Flowers (*page 94*), working straight sts with White.

Make three Small Daisies (*page 96*), working Centers with Yellow.

With Rose, make three Small Roses (*page 97*).

Sew Flowers to Sides of purse as desired.

Wildflowers

Ranunculus

Rose

Headbands

Choose from three headband designs to keep flyaways in place or just to jazz up your 'do. You can go subtle, big, or bigger—whatever suits your hair or mood!

Yarn (Medium Weight)

Wildflowers
- Band (Brown): 16 yards (14.5 meters)
- White: 16 yards (14.5 meters)
- Pink: 12 yards (11 meters)
- Green: 8 yards (7.5 meters)
- Light Blue: 8 yards (7.5 meters)
- Gold: 6 yards (5.5 meters)
- Light Green: 4 yards (3.5 meters)

Ranunculus
- Band (Brown): 16 yards (14.5 meters)
- Ecru: 12 yards (11 meters)
- Green: 4 yards (3.5 meters)

Rose
- Pink: 19 yards (17.5 meters)
- Band (Light Grey): 16 yards (14.5 meters)
- Ecru: 12 yards (11 meters)
- Olive: 9 yards (8 meters)
- Light Olive: 7 yards (6.5 meters)

Crochet Hook

- Size G (4 mm)

Additional Supplies

- Yarn needle
- Polyester fiberfill (for Wildflowers Headband)

Gauge Information

Gauge is not of great importance; your Flowers and Leaves may be a little larger or smaller without changing the overall effect.

 **EASY**

Finished Size: Band is approximately 12" (30.5 cm) long

band

With Band color, ch 42.

Row 1: 2 Hdc in third ch from hook, hdc in each ch across to last ch, 4 hdc in last ch; working in free loops of beginning ch *(Fig. 3, page 15)*, hdc in next 38 chs, 2 hdc in next ch, slip st in next ch, ch 70; finish off.

Join Band color with slip st at opposite end; ch 70, finish off.

wildflowers

Using Light Blue, make two 5-Petal Flowers *(page 94)*, working straight sts with White.

Using Pink, make one Ranunculus *(page 95)*.

Make two Small Daisies *(page 96)*.

Using Green, make two Small Leaves *(page 99)*.

Using Light Green, make one Small Leaf *(page 99)*.

Using photo as a guide for placement, sew Flowers and Leaves to Band.

ranunculus

Using Ecru, make one Ranunculus *(page 95)*.

Using Green, make one Small Leaf *(page 99)*.

Using photo as a guide for placement, sew Flower and Leaf to Band.

rose

With Ecru, make one Ranunculus *(page 95)*.

With Pink, make one Large Rose *(page 97)*.

With Olive, make one Small Leaf *(page 99)*.

With Olive, make one Large Leaf *(page 99)*.

With Light Olive, make one Laurel Leaf *(page 100)*.

Using photo as a guide for placement, sew Flowers and Leaves to Band.

Yarn GUIDE

If you want to re-create what you see by matching colors and make the projects as easily as possible, you'll want to follow our yarn guide!

In this section are the specific yarns used to create the photography models. Because yarn manufacturers make frequent changes to their product lines, you may sometimes find it necessary to use a substitute yarn or to search for the discontinued product at alternate suppliers (locally or online).

The projects in this book were all made using medium-weight yarn. You can use any brand. It is best to refer to the yardage/meters when determining how many balls or skeins to purchase. Remember, to arrive at the finished size, it is the gauge/tension that is important, not the brand of the yarn.

COASTER SET
Lily® Sugar 'n Cream®
Green: #00084 Sage Green
Light Green: #01222 Country Green
Tan: #00082 Jute
Peach: #01699 Tangerine
Light Peach: #00042 Tea Rose
White: #00001 White

DISH SCRUBBER
Lily® Sugar 'n Cream®
Green: #01222 Country Green
Peach: #01699 Tangerine

SUCCULENT GARDEN
Lion Brand® Vanna's Choice®
White: #100 White
Grey: #150 Pale Grey
Fern: #171 Fern
Brown: #126 Chocolate
Sweet Pea: #169 Sweet Pea
Kelly Green: #172 Kelly Green
Sage: #177 Sage
Yellow: #159 Lemon

CACTUS PENCIL CUP HOLDER
Red Heart® Super Saver®
Green: #0406 Medium Thyme
Pink: #0706 Perfect Pink

POTHOLDER
Lily® Sugar 'n Cream®
Green: #01222 Country Green
Grey: #01042 Overcast
Peach: #00042 Tea Rose
White: #00001 White

PRICKLY PEAR CACTUS
Lion Brand® Vanna's Choice®
Green: #171 Fern
Navy: #110 Navy
Brown: #403 Barley
Light Green: #169 Sweet Pea
Yellow: #159 Lemon

SAGUARO CACTUS
Lion Brand® Vanna's Choice®
Green: #172 Kelly Green
Grey: #149 Silver Grey
Brown: #403 Barley
Rose: #114 Cheery Cherry

SPIRAL SUCCULENT
Lion Brand® Vanna's Choice®
White: #100 White
Brown: #403 Barley
Sage: #177 Sage
Green: #173 Dusty Green

TABLE RUNNER
Lion Brand® Vanna's Choice®
Grey: #099 Linen
Sweet Pea: #169 Sweet Pea
Dusty Green: #173 Dusty Green
Sage: #177 Sage
Olive: #174 Olive
Seaspray Mist: #304 Seaspray Mist
Fern: #171 Fern
Purple: #146 Dusty Purple

ROUND CACTUS
Lion Brand® Vanna's Choice®
Rust: #135 Rust
Green: #172 Kelly Green
Brown: #403 Barley
Rose: #140 Dusty Rose

SUCCULENT SCRUBBER
Lily® Sugar 'n Cream®
Variegated: #24222 Aloe Vera
Grey: #01042 Overcast

TRINKET BOWL
Red Heart® Super Saver®
Green: #0661 Frosty Green
Pink: #0259 Flamingo
White: #0311 White

ANTLER WALL HANGING
Lion Brand® Vanna's Choice®
Linen: #099 Linen
Pink: #101 Pink
Grey: #149 Silver Grey
Light Blue: #105 Silver Blue
Light Olive: #173 Dusty Green
Olive: #174 Olive
White: #100 White

WREATH

Lion Brand® Vanna's Choice®
Linen: #099 Linen
Light Olive: #173 Dusty Green
Pink: #101 Pink
Ecru: #098 Fisherman
Rose: #142 Rose
Gold: #158 Mustard
White: #100 White
Light Blue: #105 Silver Blue
Green: #172 Kelly Green
Light Green: #171 Fern
Olive: #174 Olive

GARLAND

Red Heart® Soft®
Rose: #9770 Rose Blush
Off White: #4601 Off White
Green: #9522 Leaf

BURLAP & FLOWERS

Red Heart® Soft®
Light Gold: #9114 Honey
Off White: #4601 Off White
Green: #9522 Leaf
Dark Green: #9523 Dk Leaf
Rose: #9770 Rose Blush

DREAMCATCHER
Lion Brand® Vanna's Choice®
White: #100 White
Light Grey: #150 Pale Grey
Pink: #101 Pink
Light Rose: #140 Dusty Rose
Taupe: #125 Taupe
Light Olive: #173 Dusty Green
Olive: #174 Olive

BARRETTES
Lion Brand® Vanna's Choice®
Daisy
Green: #172 Kelly Green
Gold: #158 Mustard
White: #100 White
Light Green: #171 Fern
Flower Bouquet
Pink: #101 Pink
Light Olive: #173 Dusty Green
Ecru: #098 Fisherman
Light Blue: #105 Silver Blue
Olive: #174 Olive
White: #100 White
Mum
Rose: #142 Rose
Light Olive: #173 Dusty Green
Olive: #174 Olive

FLORAL COWL
Lion Brand® Wool-Ease®
Main Color: #403 Mushroom
Contrasting Color: #098 Fisherman

DAISY PURSE
Lion Brand® Vanna's Choice®
Main Color: #099 Linen
White: #100 White
Gold: #158 Mustard
Light Green: #171 Fern

DRAWSTRING PURSE
Red Heart® Soft®
Green: #9522 Leaf
Taupe: #9274 Biscuit
Rose: #9770 Rose Blush
White: #4600 White
Aqua: #9520 Seafoam
Yellow: #4616 Lemon

HEADBANDS
Lion Brand® Vanna's Choice®
Wildflowers
Brown: #403 Barley
White: #100 White
Pink: #101 Pink
Green: #172 Kelly Green
Light Blue: #105 Silver Blue
Gold: #158 Mustard
Light Green: #171 Fern
Ranunculus
Brown: #403 Barley
Ecru: #098 Fisherman
Green: #172 Kelly Green
Rose
Pink: #101 Pink
Light Grey: #150 Pale Grey
Ecru: #098 Fisherman
Olive: #174 Olive
Light Olive: #173 Dusty Green

Amy Gaines is a well-known amigurumi designer, selling both knit and crochet patterns online to crafters around the world. Amy started her first shop on Etsy in 2006 and now can also be found on Ravelry, Craftsy, Amazon, LoveKnitting, and Creative Fabrica. Amy's patterns have been published in many magazines, including *Vogue Knitting*, *Knit 1*, *Elle Italia*, and *Crochet!* Amy's work can also be found in several Leisure Arts pattern books, including *Cute Little Animals* and *Little Knitted Creatures*. Amy was featured on the PBS program *Knit and Crochet Now* and in several Bluprint instructional videos. Amy also designs patterns for Lion Brand Yarn. The Massachusetts resident credits her husband Chris and her two daughters, Audrey and Alice, for their help and inspiration.

index

Note: Page numbers in *italics* indicate projects, and page numbers in parentheses indicate project-specific yarn details (*see also* p. 153).

BETTER DAY BOOKS®
HAPPY • CREATIVE • CURATED

Business is personal at Better Day Books. We were founded on the belief that all people are creative and that making things by hand is inherently good for us. It's important to us that you know how much we appreciate your support. The book you are holding in your hands was crafted with the artistic passion of the author and brought to life by a team of wildly enthusiastic creatives who believed it could inspire you. If it did, please drop us a line and let us know about it. Connect with us on Instagram, post a photo of your art, and let us know what other creative pursuits you are interested in learning about. It all matters to us. You're kind of a big deal.

it's a good day to have a better day!

www.betterdaybooks.com
better_day_books